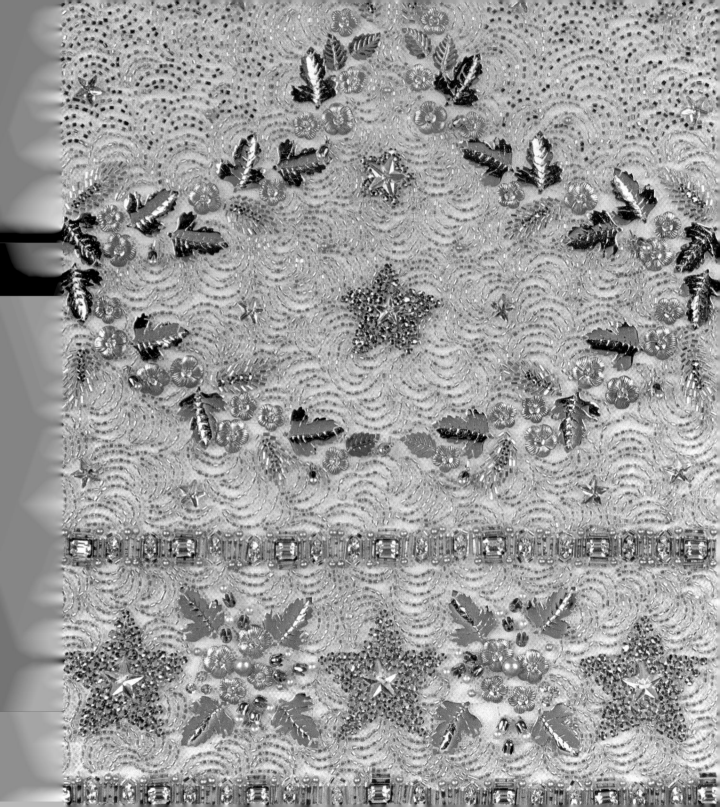

The Queen's Clothes

Illustrations by *Robb*
Text by Anne Edwards

Introduction by
Sir Norman Hartnell, K.C.V.O.

An **EXPRESS** Book

in association with Elm Tree Books

This book was designed and produced
by the Rainbird Publishing Group Limited,
36 Park Street, London W1Y 4DE
for Beaverbrook Newspapers Limited,
Fleet Street, London EC4A 2NJ

Editor and picture researcher: Mary Anne Sanders
Designer: Yvonne Dedman
Production: Elizabeth Leksinski

Printed and bound by
W. S. Cowell Ltd, Ipswich, Suffolk

SBN 241 89709 2

This book was distributed by Elm Tree Books Limited
90 Great Russell Street, London WC1B 3PT

Contents

(reverse of frontispiece) *Embroidery on the dress worn for the State visit to Iran in 1961 (see page 68). The slim-fitting dress in heavy dull silk was embroidered from neck to hem with this design in emerald and crystal. In the centre of each diamante-edged leaf hangs a pear-drop emerald bead swinging from three diamante beads, an echo of the cabochon emeralds which the Queen wears in her emerald and diamond tiara. At the top of each of these motifs is a crystal circle with five emerald drops and one large round emerald jewel bead encircled by diamante.*

(frontispiece) *Embroidery on the dress worn for the State visit to Italy in 1961 (see page 68). In shades of gold and amber and topaz the rich embroidery covered the bodice, shaded to a delicate scatter of silver and then deepened to rich gold round the hem. The theme of stars and oakleaves is carried out in topaz jewels, amber pearls, gold beads and gold thread with a sprinkling of white pearls and diamante. The richness of the embroidery is increased by the raised golden oakleaves, the raised pearly flowers, and the big square-cut topaz jewel beads. Each flower has its jewelled stamen, each leaf its jewelled spine, each topaz its jewelled frame and the feathery fronds are embroidered in tiny gold and crystal bugles. This intricate embroidery was worked on net mounted on heavy silk.*

Illustrations

Introduction

It was worth the effort of climbing up those flights of stairs to arrive, sky-high, in the well-mannered comfort of the apartment of Andrew Robb.

Although an artist of world repute, he is innocent of conceit, affectation or pretentiousness, and greets one with rare and enjoyable charm. Swiftly one is ushered into a large living room, decorated in tones of coffee, toffee and mustard, proffered a staunch whisky in a cut glass shaped like a thistle – (Scottish!), and soon the pure pleasures of social intercourse are accompanied by much jolly bonhomie and badinage.

He is full of common sense and some uncommon sense. Insomuch as he quickly turned to the important subject on hand, the contents and production of this very book.

'The idea is,' he said, 'to reproduce my already published sketches of the dresses you have designed for H.M. the Queen along with *these*!' – and he led me to a wall covered with framed motifs of the embroideries I had used in the creation of the royal dresses.

I must explain here that on several occasions when Robb had published a sketch of some special State dress in the *Daily Express*, with gracious permission from Buckingham Palace and the enthusiasm of the Editor, I had rewarded him with a 'sample' in the form of a square of satin or suchlike material, embroidered with a similar motif as that of the illustrated dress. These had all been mounted and framed, and now they hung there brilliantly illuminated, a coruscating galaxy of breathtaking beauty.

In November 1947 the *Daily Express* was in touch with me asking if their artist, Robb, could sketch the wedding dress I was to provide for the marriage of H.R.H. Princess Elizabeth to Lieutenant Philip Mountbatten, on the understanding that nothing would be published until the morning of the ceremony. Buckingham Palace had given permission to do this.

Under these strained circumstances I met Robb and revealed to him my drawings. Mutual trust was established then, and I must say that, on many similar occasions, a bond of observance of secrecy, etiquette and protocol has been maintained ever since.

The design was composed of pearls upon satin. That eminent historian, Mr James Laver, said that 'the occasion demanded a poet, and Mr Hartnell has not failed to string his lyre with art and to ring in tune'.

Well, that was the first time Robb reproduced a design of mine in the famous paper he still works for. So many more followed. Amongst them, for Canada, was the maple leaf in green velvet and emeralds on pale green; for Australia the yellow mimosa (or wattle); for France the *fleurs des champs* – gold with Napoleon's busy bee in brown chenille; for the Vatican jet and diamonds on black lace with a veil for an audience with the Pope; for Pakistan emerald beads and diamonds and for Japan a mist of pink cherry-blossom cascading down a backcloth of azure chiffon. And in another all the emblems of Great Britain and the Commonwealth clustered together upon the dress I designed for Her Majesty's Coronation.

They hang there not as a memoir of ephemeral fashion but as a reminder of the historic significance of all the great State visits, so dutifully undertaken by our beloved monarch Her Majesty the Queen.

Norman Hartnell, December 1976

Sir Norman Hartnell, k.c.v.o.

Robb's sketch of Norman Hartnell showing his designs to the Queen

Foreword

It all began with a blank wall. When I moved to a new flat recently, the decoration was complete except for one long wall in my sitting-room.

It was then that I had the idea that here was the ideal opportunity to display my unique collection of exquisite embroideries. These embroideries are samples of the motifs which adorned fifteen of the Queen's dresses all designed by Norman Hartnell, which were worked by the same team in Hartnell's salon that laboured so painstakingly on the actual dresses. Starting with the wedding dress and including the Coronation dress, they showed in close-up the detail and their full beauty.

So I had the embroideries, some on satin, some on lace and some on net, all carefully mounted, framed and hung. The result is a stunningly beautiful wall, shimmering with colour. Each is delicately lighted by carefully focused spotlights. But it is more. It is a history of the magnificence and the significance of the Queen's clothes. Here is a detailed record of the dresses she had worn on her wedding day, at her Coronation and on some of her worldwide State and official visits.

I talked to my agent Dennis Bosdet of Linden Artists, and we agreed that the collection ought to have a permanent record in book form, not only because it would interest so many but also because it should have a place in the history of royal fashion. The next move was to contact a publisher.

Michael Rainbird of the Rainbird Publishing Group, an old friend of my agent, was invited to see the collection and was immediately enthusiastic. He felt it should form the essence of a book on the Queen's clothes covering the whole of her life.

Having worked for over forty years for Beaverbrook Newspapers I immediately put the idea of this book to them using my collection of what I call 'The Royal Embroideries' as the heart of it. By 9 o'clock the following morning, Brian Nicholson, Joint Deputy Managing Director of Beaverbrook Newspapers had telephoned me and by 11 am he had seen the collection and that same afternoon he had decided to publish in time to celebrate the Queen's Jubilee. This meant immediate activity for all concerned.

This book on the Queen's clothes includes some of the many drawings which I have done for the *Daily* and *Sunday Express* over the years, together with an accompanying text by Anne Edwards and some one hundred photographs. Anne needs no introduction and has been my colleague since we first covered Paris and London fashions after the War and I am very grateful for her hard work and co-operation in this unique venture.

I had never planned to make a collection as such, and if it surprised me when I saw it framed, and lit up on the wall, it certainly staggered Norman.

It is thanks to Mary Anne Sanders, who keeps herself very much in the background and who edited the book, to Michael Rainbird, and to Brian Nicholson for the enthusiasm he has shown, that we have something which may add to the history of our fashion history.

Robb, January 1977

1
Salad Days

From the day she was christened in a robe of Honiton lace which had been worn by her father, her grandfather and her great-grandfather, the future Queen had less freedom of choice in what she wore than many of her subjects. There were so many restrictions, even though cost was not among them. The formality which distinguishes all that the Queen wears is part of a pattern set in childhood before it was anticipated that she would inherit the crown, and reinforced when this became inevitable.

Sheltered and protected in nursery and schoolroom, restricted to mixing only with children from the same upper-class background, obedient to the decisions of her parents and grandmamma, from her baby days she lived the formal, regulated life then considered suitable in wealthy, aristocratic British families.

Nanny-dressed in the nanny tradition of party dresses from Fortnum & Mason and velvet-collared coats and gaiters from Hayters or Debenham & Freebody she, like the other children in her set, wore the kind of clothes that only Nanny's charges could afford.

There were tailored wool coats with dozens of buttons which needed Nanny to do them up, smocked and pintucked dresses which fastened at the back so Nanny must be there to put them on, short frilly party dresses in organdie and net which needed Nanny to press them every time they were worn, and knee length white socks which Nanny would launder.

In summer the children wore little straw brimmed hats trimmed with a wreath of flowers and in winter a fancy beret to match their pale wool coats, which Nanny would take to be cleaned. Shoes were always the sensible one-bar or lace-up variety in serviceable calf for daytime, and silver kid pumps for parties. Playing in the grounds of Windsor or Sandringham the nearest they ever got to informality was a pleated tartan skirt and shetland wool sweater.

Princess Elizabeth in tweed jacket and check skirt at the age of fourteen with one of the corgis.

"one ride on a tube"

Oddly enough when so much else has changed on the fashion scene, in this one area of dressing the children of the well-heeled British still wear the same styles that the Queen wore fifty years ago, and will probably continue to do so as long as Nanny is there to do the shopping.

The Queen's own children followed the pattern until they were allowed to go to school where they mixed with other children not of their set, wore the same school uniform as the others, learned the superior advantages of trousers, shirts and bulky sweaters, and where they were allowed to take part in so many activities which were denied their mother.

When the mini-skirt became fashionable Princess Anne wore her skirts at mid-thigh length. Had the Queen been a girl at the time of that fashion it would have taken a palace revolution to permit her to wear them.

A comparison of the Queen's upbringing with that of her children gives some idea of the limitations imposed on her, limitations which inevitably restricted an interest in fashion as well as the choice of clothes.

She was only ten years old when she became the direct heir to the throne, and from then on the pressure to conform to upper-class formality combined with the pressure to dress with regal formality too.

Less than any other girl in her realm did she have the chance to learn how to dress, to copy other girls, to make wild mistakes and learn from them, to develop a personal style and indulge a personal taste.

From the schoolroom with Miss Marion Crawford as governess and specially selected fellow pupils she went on to solitary lessons from a tutor, Henry Marten, the Provost of Eton. When she became a girl guide in 1939 it was the special Buckingham Palace Company of Girl Guides in which she enrolled, and when she joined the A.T.S. during the war she returned home to Windsor every night for dinner, bed and breakfast.

Her sole excursions into rubbing shoulders with the crowd are said to be one ride on a tube, from St James's

(above left) Princess Elizabeth, not yet a year old, and one of the few babies who did not look like Sir Winston Churchill. In an elaborate outfit which presaged the elaborate dresses to come, the baby wears a bonnet of ruched lace edged with white swansdown and tied with a silken bow, and an elaborately embroidered collar on a coat with the finicky buttons she was later, as Queen, to find too time consuming.

(above) The Princess at five and a half wears a long dress and a white bunny-rabbit cloak with a wreath on her hair for the wedding of Lady May Cambridge and Captain Henry Abel Smith at St Mary's Church, Balcombe in Sussex.

(left) At the age of just seven the Princess begins to learn the art of shaking hands graciously. Beside her, almost identically dressed as usual is her sister. Here she is being greeted on her arrival at Olympia.

(opposite) Typical of the play clothes worn by the sisters are these short wool jerseys with ribbed neck, cuffs and waist worn over a tartan kilt with white socks and lace up low-heeled calf shoes. This picture was taken in the garden of Royal Lodge Windsor when the future Queen was ten.

Park via Charing Cross to Tottenham Court Road and back, and joining the crowd outside the Palace on V.E. day. She went occasionally to the theatre and very rarely dined in a restaurant.

As a child she and her sister were always dressed alike wearing identical dresses in identical colours with identical coats and hats. The only differences were that Princess Elizabeth's hair was parted on the right, and Princess Margaret's on the left, and that Princess Elizabeth wore a triple row of pearls in her necklet while Princess Margaret's pearls were a double row.

At the Coronation of their father they wore identical long white lace dresses with a row of bows down the front and identical lightweight coronets.

Such conformity is not likely to encourage an individual taste in dress, and there were other limitations.

Until several years after her marriage to Prince Philip, it was Princess Elizabeth's mother's taste which prevailed, with strict supervision from her father, and advice from her grandmother Queen Mary. As a teenager the Queen had dresses made largely by Miss Ford, who used to work for Handley Seymour, the firm which made Queen Mary's clothes. In those days, in any case, fashion was set by the parents' generation, and girls of eighteen tried to look thirty. It was not until many years later that mothers took their fashion cue from daughters, instead of the other way round.

The Queen Mother has always had a weakness for imposing hats, presumably on the theory that they give her height. She has always favoured hats with important-looking brims, or loaded with feathers and flowers and bows, and indeed these fluttery, feathery concoctions do suit her. For many years Princess Elizabeth followed suit, and her hats were topped with huge velvet bows, or mammoth roses, or an outsize daisy, a feather pom-pom or even a whole bird, and they were made by the same milliner, a charming Dane with an impossible name, Aage Thaarup.

The Queen Mother loved furs, especially fox-fur stoles and short fur capes. So the Princess wore them too. The Queen Mother favoured peep-toe shoes, so did her

Now aged ten, the year in which the Duke of Windsor abdicated and the Princess became heir to the throne, she is still lovingly protected by her parents. Pictured in the gardens of their home at 145 Piccadilly, with corgi dogs which she has loved all her life, she wears a printed summer dress with white pleated collar and shoulder sleeves.

daughter. The Queen Mother likes shiny taffetas and satin, rich velvet and soft crepe even in day time, and draped bodices with skirts that are neither quite straight nor very full. It would have been considered indelicate to outline her figure and in any case it did not become her. And although these fashions were current in the forties, the royal ladies continued to wear them long after Dior's New Look had outdated them, and the little Princess like other daughters continued to dress like a woman twice her age.

The most successful of the Queen Mother's clothes was the distinctive style of evening dress for which she became famous. This was an off-the-shoulder bodice with a swathed fichu neckline, a tight waist and an immensely full, often crinoline, skirt covered with sparkles. This style was suggested by her husband King George VI when he led Norman Hartnell to a Winter-halter painting in Buckingham Palace and asked Norman Hartnell to design something similar for the Queen.

But the Queen Mother was nearly thirty-seven when her husband was crowned. Elizabeth was twenty-five when she became Queen. So that the styles which suited her mother so well had the effect of making her daughter look matronly. The photographs of the Queen in 1948, when she was only twenty-two, show the appealing contrast between the girl and the clothes, the heavy important outlines of the dress and hat entirely failing to overwhelm the youthful charm of her face.

Yet another of the Royal traditions inherited by the Queen was the preference for pale pastel colours, initiated by Queen Mary in her silver-greys and creamy beige lace dresses, carried on by the Queen Mother in her pale pinks and pastel blues.

Richard Dimbleby, the arch-royal-commentator, so often described the Queen as wearing powder blue that it was a justified joke in the famous send up of royal commentating on the television programme 'That Was The Week That Was', when the platform on which the Royal Family stood was imagined to have sunk. 'The Queen smiling radiantly in powder blue' ran the commentary 'is swimming for her life'.

In defence of the long royal preference for pale colours it must be said that it made them easy to pick

(left) First intimations of the royal role in store for her. Princess Elizabeth now next in line for the throne, wears a childish replica of her parents' coronation robes to wave to the populace from Buckingham Palace on the occasion of her father's coronation in 1937.

(opposite) Two little girls always dressed alike photographed in the park at Windsor. They wear the same pink skirts and boleros, similar pink and white blouses with Peter Pan collars edged with white frills, identical natural-straw hats, identical light-tan one-strap, button-up shoes. As a concession to her age (she was then fifteen), Princess Elizabeth has stockings instead of white socks, and wears a silver bracelet while her sister has blue beads. This pattern of conformity was then the rule for the sisters, when Mother set the style, Nanny ordered the clothes, and teenage girls were required to look like little girls.

out in a crowd, particularly in the drab post-war period, that they are perhaps regal in their evidence of 'conspicuous consumption' on account of the cleaning bills, and that when Norman Hartnell dressed the whole family for Ascot, grouped in the Royal Box they looked like a delicate bunch of sweet peas.

Another result of the Queen's special position which should be taken into account in any assessment of her clothes is that for most of her life she has been totally immune from criticism.

She was immune not only from the self-criticism which comes from measuring yourself in your youth against more sophisticated, more elegant girls – for these were not heir presumptive to the throne of England and did not have to bear in mind their unique standing, but also from the occasional catty comment, for no one in her circle would presume to make a critical remark, least of all her dressmakers.

Even today, when she is more informal, more sure of herself, more adventurous, and more elegant, not one of the people who make her clothes would venture an even mildly deprecating comment on her choice. 'We do not dress the Queen' one of them said, 'she orders clothes from us'. Not one of them would dare to suggest that she might carry rather smaller and more fashionable handbags or dictate what shoes should go with which outfit, nor even suggest except in the subtlest way (such as making an emerald-green evening dress) that she

With her marriage sixteen months ahead, and the engagement not to be announced until she was twenty-one, Princess Elizabeth poses for a formal photograph at Buckingham Palace. Looking still very unsophisticated, much younger than her years (she was just over twenty when this picture was taken), still with the same hairstyle she wore as a child, still a little plump, and still wearing the royal pastel colours, the Princess about to be married and one day to be Queen wears an extremely simple dress in pale lilac crepe. It has the padded shoulders which were a hangover from the military style of wartime years, a skirt which fits closely over her always slender hips and a loose tucked bodice. Her jewels, modest for the Heir to the Throne, are a double strand pearl necklace, pearl studs and the silver bracelet she wore as a fifteen year old.

should wear her emeralds with it rather than her rubies. The dress, made for her state visit to Iran in 1961 (see p. 68), embroidered with emerald drop beads was a clear statement – and she did wear with it her diamond tiara with pear-shaped emeralds.

Nor even though they may design a particular outfit with a particular occasion in mind is there any guarantee that she will wear it then. 'She plays it by ear' they explain. 'It depends on the weather, on her mood, on what sort of clothes the other guests will be wearing'.

And though their sketch may suggest a particular hat for each outfit, it is only recently, since her milliners began to work more closely with her dress designers, that there is any guarantee that this is the hat she will choose.

The furthest in critical comment of her choice that any fitter, vendeuse or designer would dare to go would be to say 'I don't like this material, Ma'am, it creases badly. Let's get rid of it', or 'May we try this pocket a little higher, Ma'am?'.

Anyone who thinks they can get away with deliberately omitting a detail from an accepted design is reminded that the Queen has a fantastic memory, a marvellous eye for detail, that she notices everything and forgets nothing.

It is not that she is ever curt or discourteous. Everyone who works for her testifies to her considerate charm, and she for her part never criticizes their work. But she has a manner which does not brook argument and is said to have in her armoury a look which can kill at twenty paces.

To this total immunity from criticism has been added, for most of her life, an over-zealous protectiveness from her previous press office, who regarded even a request to know the colour of the dress the Queen had worn as an intrusion into her privacy and thereby alienated most fashion writers, as well as a treacly form of flattery from commentators and writers of books on royalty.

It is almost impossible in today's freer and friendlier atmosphere between royalty and the people to realize

Already at nine years old the Princess makes her public appearance wearing hat and gloves, at the celebration of her grandmother's Silver Jubilee. The picture shows three generations of the royal family on the balcony at Buckingham Palace. On the right is the elegant Princess Marina in pale grey, wearing the large picture hat style which is taboo for British royalty.

The Princess in neat little tweed coat with velvet collar and beret to match, gloves and lace-up shoes, so formally dressed even for taking her corgi for a walk in Hyde Park when she was only ten.

The only picture ever published of Princess Elizabeth in a swim-suit revealing a figure better than most of the team's. Taken at the Bath Club when she was a member of a team for the challenge cup and thirteen years old.

in what sickening and servile terms every aspect of the Royal Family's life was usually described. Even a man as intelligent as Richard Dimbleby found nothing absurd in rapturizing over Prince Charles's skill in dancing class; and in a book on *Our Princesses and their Dogs*, which is entirely devoted to the little girls and their corgis, the captions to the photographs are in this humble prose: 'If to the Duke and Duchess of York it is a matter of pride that their children possess such sunny natures and such sunny smiles, it must equally be a matter of deep satisfaction to their dogs.'

Not until she was thirty did the first outspoken attacks come and the press begin to alter its tone. She had been four years on the throne before Lord Altrincham wrote publicly the criticisms which some had voiced in private. Directing his caustic comments on the young Queen's image at those who prepared her speeches he wrote that 'The personality conveyed by the utterances which are put into her mouth is that of a priggish schoolgirl, captain of the hockey team, a prefect and a recent candidate for confirmation' . . . 'Her entourage are mostly of the tweedy sort' . . . 'The Queen's style of speaking is a pain in the neck'.

This image had not been helped by her conservative style of dress which gave the impression of a little girl wearing her mother's dresses and which also should have been blamed on the example of the social set which surrounded her.

Although this attack made some of her entourage purple with rage it did her better service than the uncritical adulation which had swaddled her until then.

It was clear to close followers of the royal progress that like a true professional dedicated to do her work to the best of her ability, she took note of the criticism,

lowered the pitch of her voice, and improved her fashion image.

To imagine that the Queen with a huge dress account, a vast new wardrobe every year, the country's best designers to call upon, hundreds of social occasions on which to show off her clothes surrounded by admiring crowds, is living in a feminine paradise is wide of the mark.

She has never until very recently been much interested in clothes. 'She is too intelligent' says one of her designers 'to be a fanatic about fashion'. Only her rigid sense of duty can have prevented the yearly preparation of so many clothes from turning the procedure into a business chore.

When on holiday or at home she wears comfortable tweed jackets and wool skirts and twin sets, or plain simple day dresses in wool or cotton or silk, and she is

(left) *The two princesses dressed alike for riding, and again* (right) *when Princess Elizabeth made her first broadcast in 1940. An indication of how plainly they were dressed in their teens is that the same clothes turn up in many of their posed photographs. At home at Royal Lodge, Windsor, with her horse in 1943 (overleaf left), and with her family in 1946, (overleaf right) she wears simple printed cotton dresses.*

The first in a long series of uniforms is her Guide uniform. Later were to come her A.T.S. uniform and then as Queen the uniform of Colonel of the Grenadier Guards at Trooping the Colour and the mantles and robes of the Garter, the Order of the Bath, of St Michael and St George, and of the Thistle.

(right) Typical of the influence of wartime uniform on fashion is this tweed suit cut on military lines worn with a tweed hat which is a version of the service cap. Here, at sixteen, after becoming Colonel of the Grenadier Guards, the Princess wears the grenade cap badge of an officer in her hat.

At eighteen the heir to the throne still looks remarkably young and unsophisticated. Here at her desk in Windsor Castle she wears a print dress with bows on the sleeves and neckline, with a gold wrist watch and two-strand pearl necklace.

obviously happy and relaxed in a raincoat and head-scarf.

Secondly, she has never until recently had the ideal figure for wearing fashionable dresses, or the assurance to carry them off. The ideal fashion-plate figure is at least 5 ft 9 in. tall, painfully thin and without curves. The Princess, 5 ft 3 in. tall, and plump after the birth of her first baby, retired shyly behind swathed necklines, bouquets resolutely held front on, and generally full skirts.

Thirdly, the upbringing and background which conditioned her to the conservative style of the upper-class British (which an American once described as 'dowdy-chic') is not the best training ground for high fashion. The views of her parents had always been the deciding factor and those who thought that Prince Philip would have an influence did not know Prince Philip.

In the tradition of his class at that time, most husbands thought it unmanly to know about fashion and unmannerly to criticize a woman's dress, and to this day Prince Philip has never attended a fitting and never been known to express a view on the Queen's clothes except that he doesn't like her to wear big hats.

Fourthly, by far the biggest factor in choosing clothes is the suitability for the job. This imposes a strict formula.

To appreciate the importance of clothes to the efficient performance of her job, it is essential to understand some aspects of her role which are taken for granted.

Apart from State business the Queen's job is to be seen and seen by millions of people not only in Britain but all over the world.

Except for the few who demand a cut-price monarchy or no monarchy at all, the majority of people feel that the Queen is doing a good job and recognize that while she is doing it she should dress the part.

Everyone realizes that this entails wearing a great many clothes and expensive clothes at that, since no one would be more disappointed than her subjects if she took to wearing chain-store clothes or the same ready-made as their next-door neighbour. Everyone, too,

The first picture of Princess Elizabeth and Philip taken after the announcement of their engagement when she was twenty-one shows her wearing the favourite royal pastel colours, the favourite pearls, and the favourite loosely draped bodice. She wears her diamond engagement ring for the first time.

feels free to criticize her clothes, especially the French and American fashion writers, without appreciating the reasons why she chooses the clothes she wears, which subordinate private taste to professional demands.

What most people do not realize is that every single

Six weeks before her engagement was announced Princess Elizabeth visited the Queen Elizabeth Hospital for children in Hackney. Already the first sign of royal dressing is apparent in the imposing hat trimmed with a bunch of lily-of-the-valley and the almond-green jacket and dress with white gloves and handbag.

A few days before her marriage the Princess even more formally dressed than before visits the headquarters of the Grenadier Guards in Buckingham Gate to see the wedding presents that the regiment was giving her. Clearly influenced by her mother's taste she wears a hat with feather-wings, a square-shouldered pastel wool coat, gloves and clutch handbag, with pearls and the regimental brooch. But the shoes are still in the sensible lace-up style of her early teens.

With the radiant look of a girl who is in love Princess Elizabeth on one of her solo appearances wears the royal pastel in a coat with the cross-over line supposed to be slimming, and a forerunner of the breton hats she found so ideal in later years.
The pearls, the shoulder brooch, the gloves are here, but inexperienced as yet in hand shaking and bouquet receiving she has a clutch bag under her arm.

Three royal ladies reflect the taste of the Queen Mother; all three in pastel and pearls with discreetly draped bodices and pale low-heeled shoes. Her mother's taste influenced Elizabeth's choice of clothes until long after she became Queen.

The announcement of her engagement aroused so much interest that Elizabeth appeared on the balcony at Buckingham Palace with Philip in response to the cheering crowds who had gathered. The Princess wears a pale blue crepe dress with padded shoulders and bead embroidery round the waist and on the bolero, which is typical of the era.

31

detail of every single thing she wears is planned and programmed for a unique job. The length of her hem, the width of her skirt, the shape of her neckline, the height of her heels, the make of her gloves, the design of her hats and her coats, the style of her handbags, the fabrics and the colours are all dictated by her work.

For these reasons she has never been, never wanted to be and never could be a fashion leader. Not since Princess Marina popularised the pill-box hat has any Royal lady set a fashion. And for these reasons she can be accused of looking a little unadventurous, but equally she has never, even looking back through the years, looked ridiculous as so many fashion leaders look now, viewed with hindsight.

One other point which escapes the fashion critics is that it is unthinkable that the Queen should pose, except in the most formal line-ups, for a picture.

Anyone who has worked in fashion photography knows the tricks: the special lighting, the angle always from below to give an elongated effect, the three-quarter stance which turns the hips slightly to look slimmer than nature, the aloof expression.

The Queen is photographed in often inelegant action, clambering up steps, leaping from ship to shore, descending the airplane gangway in a fierce wind, bending to receive a bouquet, plant a tree, or talk to a hospital patient in bed, waving, walking, pondering, inspecting, talking and recently eating – a subject long banned to photographers in the United Kingdom, on the grounds that it was impossible to look regal while chewing.

It is a tribute to the care with which her clothes are planned that this most photographed woman in the world has never been seen to hitch up a shoulder strap, tug at a hem, pat her hair, fidget with her brooch, or fuss with her hat.

And the one bonus (apart from the size of her dress allowance) on which all the designers can rely is that her complexion is so clear and pretty that she can carry off any and every colour.

The first of the historic dresses created for the Queen by Norman Hartnell was the wedding dress he made for her in 1947 when she was Princess Elizabeth. In heavy white satin exquisitely embroidered with delicate fronds and roses in pearl and crystal, the embroidery banded the neckline, the cuffs of the long tight-fitting sleeves, and the hem, and swept in graceful garlands round the skirt. For the long train in satin five petal roses outlined in pearls with centres of pearl and crystal were appliqued onto the white net, with pearl and crystal leaf fronds, repeating the embroidery on the dress. Over the train which was fastened to the shoulder was a cloud of white tulle, held by a diamond tiara. The Queen wore the pearl necklet which was a wedding present from her father and carried a bouquet of white orchids.

2
Princess in Love

Princess Elizabeth's marriage in 1947 produced the first of the memorable, exquisite, and lavish royal dresses for which Norman Hartnell has become famous. Although he made his first dress for her when she was bridesmaid to the Duchess of Gloucester, although he made many magnificent, opulent clothes for her while she was still Princess, although he has since made many beautiful dresses for her to wear on State or Commonwealth visits, there are still two dresses which above all the rest will merit a place in fashion history as important to future students as the clothes of Queen Elizabeth I are today.

"not enemy silkworms surely?"

The first of these is the Wedding Dress. The other is the Coronation Dress.

Hartnell first made clothes for the present Queen when he was requested in 1935 to make the Duchess of Gloucester's wedding dress and her bridesmaids' dresses. Among the eight bridesmaids were Princess Elizabeth and Princess Margaret Rose.

He had previously made three dresses for Queen Mary but the long connection with the Queen which began then has lasted over forty years.

It was also his first introduction to the strictures attendant on royal dressing. The designs which he made for the bridesmaids and which the Duchess approved were for sophisticated Empire-style dresses, clinging and long skirted. But King George V wished that the little Princesses should wear girlish dresses so their frocks were made short, in palest pink satin, flouncy and fluffy skirts bordered with three graduated bands of ruched pink tulle, tiny sleeves and a tulle frilled bodice.

The arrival of the family to supervise the first dress fittings is an indication of the grand style in which they were then accustomed to appear. For this visit to a dressmaker the Queen Mother, then the Duchess of York, was in silver-grey georgette with palest grey fox fur, and wore dewdrop diamonds and aquamarines. The Princesses wore little blue jackets with silver buttons and grey hats wreathed in blue forget-me-nots.

Three months later Hartnell was asked to discuss and quickly provide a few black dresses for the Duchess of York, for the court was in mourning for the death of George V in January 1936.

Then in May 1937 he was summoned to Buckingham Palace and asked to make the dresses for the Maids of Honour who would attend the new Queen at the coronation, and for the Queen herself to wear at banquets on two State visits.

These of silver tissue and silver lace, and of pearly grey satin embroidered with pearls and amethysts were the first two grand dresses which he designed for any member of the Royal Family, and from then on he dressed them all.

His training in the theatre, his marvellous gift for pageantry, his love of splendid fabrics and rich embroidery made him a natural for the job.

So it was that in 1947 when the engagement of Princess Elizabeth was announced he was summoned to the Palace to discuss dresses with the Queen her mother, and to submit sketches for the wedding dress.

His design was accepted in August and the wedding was to be on 20 November which gave him less than three months to complete the dress and train.

Some idea of the immense care and research which goes into preparing one of these royal dresses for an important occasion can be gathered from Hartnell's own record.

Embroidery on the Wedding Dress worn by Princess Elizabeth for her marriage in 1947 (see page 37). The design of five petal flowers, roses and fern fronds is worked entirely in pearl and crystal on heavy white satin. Seed pearls make the roses and outline the satin petals, a large pearl surrounded with crystal stamens makes the centre, and a pear-shaped pearl lies along each petal. The design for the white satin flower in the centre of the net panel is the one appliqued onto the net train forming a border and scattered with smaller flowers in the same design all over the train.

He began by visualizing a bridal gown of fine pearl embroidery. He went round the London art galleries in search of inspiration and found in a Botticelli figure in clinging white silk just what he sought, delicate trails of jasmine, smilax, syringa and small rose blossoms which he wanted to interpret in crystals and pearls.

For these he needed great quantities of small white American pearls, so his manager went to America and brought back ten thousand of these tiny pearls.

'Then came the problem of the satin', he writes in his autobiography. 'Her Majesty had expressed the wish that I should use a certain satin made at Lullington Castle directed by the delightful Lady Hart Dyke. This superb satin, rich lustrous and stiff, I was able to use for the lengthy train, but for the dress itself a slightly more supple material of similar tint was preferable. I ordered it from the Scottish firm of Winterthur near Dunfermline; and then the trouble started. I was told in confidence that certain circles were trying to stop the use of the Scottish satin on the grounds of patriotism; the silk worms, they said, were Italian, and possibly even Japanese! Was I so guilty of treason that I would deliberately use *enemy* silk worms?

'I telephoned through to Dunfermline, begging them to ascertain the true nationality of the worms; were they Italian worms, Japanese worms, or Chinese worms?

'Our worms' came the proud reply, 'are Chinese worms – from Nationalist China, of course'.

'After which we were able to get on with the job with a much easier conscience'.

The embroidery when it was completed bordered the hem, the long satin sleeves and neckline on the dress and swooped over the full skirt in soft garlands of pearl orange-blossom, syringa, jasmine and the white rose of York with graceful curves of wheat-ears in pearls and diamonds.

Worldwide curiosity surrounded the dress. It was reported that the design would be pirated and copies put on the market on the day of the wedding.

Hartnell's staff were offered bribes. Enterprising photographers tried to rent rooms overlooking the

(left) At twenty-one and looking wonderfully happy the Princess with Philip arrives at the theatre for the Royal Command Variety Performance. In contrast to the far grander clothes she wears on these occasions as Queen, she wears a Hartnell dress in grey and white printed satin, with a swathed fichu (so often part of the royal dress while she was still plump) in softly draped white satin. With it she has a cape in white fox, long white gloves, and double string of pearls. The Queen did not possess a tiara until she was married when Queen Mary presented her with the delicate tiara which is now the Queen's favourite.

(opposite) The wedding of Princess Elizabeth in Westminster Abbey showing the High Altar with its magnificent gold plate, the glow of candles and heavy brocade, the brass chandeliers and the ornate copes of the clergy. The Princess and her six bridesmaids made a charming contrast in their clouds of white tulle, pearls and crystal.

(*opposite left*) *Leaving Westminster Abbey after her marriage and the crowds who had waited for hours get their first glimpse of the wedding dress. A detailed description of the exquisite workmanship and design of the embroidery is on page 33.*

(*opposite right*) *This aerial view of the Queen at her wedding shows the exquisite embroidery of appliqued satin and pearl and crystal stars on the fifteen-foot train.*

(*opposite below*) *The wedding group. The bride is surrounded by her family and in-laws, her eight bridesmaids and two pages. The bridesmaids' dresses in ivory tulle are embroidered with the same satin stars as the bridal train.*

(*right*) *The Robb drawing of the wedding dress which was a world exclusive entrusted to him in advance for publication on the wedding day. Hartnell's gratitude for a sketch beautifully executed and a secret well kept in face of worldwide curiosity resulted in the gift of a panel of the embroidered fabric which began the unique collection of embroideries.*

37

workroom. Extraordinary precautions had to be taken to keep the dress a secret. The workroom windows were whitewashed and covered with thick white muslin. The manager of the salon offered to keep guard at night by sleeping in the room next to the one where the dress was kept.

On the evening of the wedding the newspapers had to content themselves with photographs of the four-foot box leaving for the Palace.

Hartnell had wisely advised against the traditional use of heavy heirloom lace to make the bridal veil and

A married woman of three months now the Princess attends a wedding at St Margaret's Church, Westminster. Carrying the clutch handbag style she was later to discard when the bouquets and the handshaking made this fashion impracticable, the Princess still bears the influence of the Queen Mother's style. Both wear similar hats with the brim swept high on the left and trimmed with a large tuft of feathers.

The Going-away Dress was, in those days, the most important item of a bride's trousseau. For hers, the Princess chose a dress and coat in airforce-blue wool with a felt hat to match trimmed with a tuft of brown feathers. At the start of her honeymoon she rides in an open landau with her new husband and the crowds throw petals on the carriage which is taking her to Waterloo for the journey to Broadlands in Hampshire.

the Princess wore the far softer, more flattering veil of white tulle which floated from a diamond tiara in a white cloud half way along her fifteen-foot train. The tiara was the 'something borrowed', traditionally supposed to bring good luck to the bride, for it belongs to her mother. The train itself was a delicate embroidery of the same flowers graduated from the shoulders towards the hem, and bordered with roses, with centres of raised pearls on silver wire thread.

The train was held by two small pages, and the bridesmaids dresses were in ivory tulle with full skirts, tight-fitting bodices and fichus of tulle with a scatter of small star-shaped blossoms embroidered in pearl and crystal like a milky way across the skirts.

The usual last-minute hitches occurred as they do at most weddings.

At the last moment when the Princess's personal maid and two of Hartnell's sewing women had already gone to the Abbey to be ready for any emergencies, when the head saleswomen had helped to dress the bride at the Palace and the bride was ready to leave, the bouquet of white orchids could not be found.

There was no one to send looking for it, for Palace staff had been given standing room in the forecourt of the Palace to see the bride leave; the King, the bride, and the saleswoman were the only people on hand.

The bride had no idea where her bouquet could be. The King had no idea either. So the saleswoman searched the corridors, then searched the huge ground-floor rooms, and finally discovered the bouquet in the porter's lodge.

Sir John Colville tells of the other emergency in his recent book *Footprints in Time*. He was the Princess's

Derby Day in June 1948 five months before Prince Charles was born, the Princess is walking down to the paddock before a race accompanied by the King. The Dior New Look had burst on the scene the previous year and the Princess wears a much modified royal version with a longer, fuller-skirted coat over a print dress, belted waist, ankle-strap shoes and a hat with a flowing veil.

Private Secretary at the time when half an hour before she was due to leave, he was summoned urgently to the Palace. There was the Princess in her sitting-room, radiant in her wedding gown and ready to leave, but the pearl necklace, given to her by her father among other jewels for her wedding, had been left with the other presents which had been put on show at St James's Palace. And the Princess had set her heart on wearing it for her wedding.

Could he fetch it for her in time? Take any car, she said, so he dashed away, leapt into the first royal Daimler he saw which happened at the time to be occupied by King Haakon of Norway arriving for the wedding, talked his way past the janitor on the door of St James's Palace, ran upstairs and told his story to the C.I.D. men guarding the presents.

It was an unlikely story, from some chap in an R.A.F. uniform who said he was the Princess's Private Secre-

tary and that she wanted him to bring her her pearl necklace. They tried to ring Buckingham Palace to check but the line was dead. They looked in the official programme and saw his name there. It could so easily have been a hoax, but what were they to do? If he was a thief, they were in trouble. If he was not and the Princess did not get her pearls in time to wear them, they were in trouble.

Finally the Senior Officer believed him, but as Sir John Colville writes: 'He must have been relieved when the evening papers appeared with photographs of the Princess in her bridal gown and wearing the pearls'.

But in the end it all went off well, reflecting on a grand scale the social ritual so well known to so many families; grandmamma upright and regal as ever in a dress and coat of golden tissue embossed with her favourite chenille in sea blue; the mother of the bride trailing apricot brocade; the groom handsome in naval uniform, and finally the bride walking serenely down the aisle in a shimmer of satin and pearl.

One year after the Princess's marriage her first child was born. Her second child was born less than two years later. The hysterical adulation which had surrounded her was now centred on her children, but with the advent of a more motherly figure combined with the long skirts of the time, criticisms of her clothes were murmured abroad. 'Frumpish' said the Americans; 'Englishwomen' said the French, 'can look pretty but never chic'.

To be fair the British clothes of the early forties are to some probably the least attractive in the whole history of fashion. In Britain there had been years of rationing and anyone not in uniform felt that they ought to be, so civvy dress followed as closely as possible military outlines of stiffened square shoulders, long jackets, and short straight skirts. It had even been a fashion during the war years to have a man's morning suit adapted for women, to make a severe black jacket and grey-and-black-striped skirt which was cut from the trousers. Few women had worn hats during the war preferring for everyday a turban of wool or silk which

(*above*) *At the Bath and West Agricultural Show in 1948 the Princess in her New Look, fuller, longer coat in heavy emerald green silk with a 'Dorothy Bag' in the same material, and a wide brimmed black hat which has a crown of flowers and a veil. Clutching one of the thousands of bouquets she has been given in her lifetime resolutely in front, she wears the usual combination of pearls and lapel brooch.*

(*opposite*) *By 1948 when this photograph was taken at the opening of new houses for employees on the royal estate in Norfolk the Princess and her sister no longer dress alike. The Queen more conservative than Princess Margaret wears the squared padded shoulder, long jacket and pleated skirt which was a wartime civvy style. Her concession to frivolity is a flowered hat with tulle veil, a style she was later to wear with more chic and a more suitable hairstyle.*

was a straight scarf twisted round and tucked in. It would have been tasteless, during the blitz, to be seen picking a way carefully over the debris wearing expensive clothes, and those women who had fur coats put them away for the duration.

Moreover, Paris, from which new fashions had come for so many years, was occupied by the Germans. It was not revealed until Paris was liberated that the fashions which the French women wore were far worse than the British, for with some subtle idea of revenge they made fashionable the ugliest clothes ever seen on European women, huge ape-like shoulders and very short skirts, topped by grotesque, chimney-pot hats.

This was not an era when elegance could flourish and the rampaging success of Dior's New Look in 1949 was due to the psychological release it afforded to women so long constricted into a uniform military style.

But every new fashion to succeed must have a balanced silhouette, it must be all or nothing, and for the New Look 'all' meant near ankle-length hemlines, vast thirty-yard skirts, tiny nipped waists, saucy little hats and very high heels. Seductive, impractical, uneconomical, uncomfortable, and anti-social because of the immense yardage at a time when materials were scarce, against all common sense it was a runaway success.

The Princess as usual could give only a passing nod in the direction of the New Look – her hems were a little longer, her skirts a little fuller, her heels a little higher.

These two photographs of the Princess with her first and second babies show how little her style of dressing changed over the intervening years. In the first, holding Prince Charles, she wears a coat in coral wool with a matching coral velvet hat trimmed with a huge velvet bow, a veil and a band of darker coral. In the second, holding Princess Anne, she wears an equally elderly print dress in no particular style with an equally important over-trimmed hat, the same pearl necklet, and different shoulder brooch – in one a bow of diamonds, in the other a sapphire surrounded in diamonds. The babies wear the same ornate lace and satin christening robes.

42

Moreover The Look was at its best in black, and the Princess traditionally rarely wore black except for evening or for mourning, although it suits her better than anything else. 'I cannot wear dark colours' she tells her dressmakers, 'it makes me one of the crowd'.

For evening she continued to wear the full-skirted, sparkling dresses she had worn all her life which were

(for the caption to the photograph opposite see overleaf)

(below) At the first of the exhausting foreign tours which she undertook with her husband the Princess went to Canada travelling twice across the continent, and visiting some seventy cities, towns, and halting points. Here she wears a coat in bottle-green velvet with a skull cap trimmed with green feathers which she wore for her arrival in Quebec. The seamed stockings date the occasion, the court shoe heels a little higher than she wears today.

undeniably regal but failed to indicate that there was a woman inside. It was not until 1957 that she broke away from this line, and for the first time wore a pencil-slim gown of silver lace over silver tissue for her night trip along the Seine on her first state visit to Paris. Such a departure from the normal made news.

It was unexpected, it was alluring, it revealed that the Queen had an excellent figure with long slender lines. It was such a success that she returned to the same slinky style later that year for two dresses which she wore on a State Visit to the U.S.A., and has returned to the slim-fitting line again and again since, to the delight particularly of her dressmakers who continue to nudge her gently into more daring clothes.

Three other examples of the rare adventurous approach are worth recording here. The first in 1952 was abortive, the second in 1953 was a mistake, the third, three years later, was a triumph, but none have ever been repeated.

The first was an attempt to get the Princess dressed by the Paris-based House of Molyneux. She ordered a couple of dresses there for her South African tour as Princess, but before she had a chance to wear them her father died, and she hurried home. Mourning clothes were quickly provided and taken to her on the 'plane so that when she stepped on to English soil she was in deep black.

Although she never wore a Molyneux dress in public, she did follow one of his designers to the humbler house of Horrocks and continued for several years to wear the simple cotton dresses which he designed.

For the other two experiments the Queen was to be at a Royal Première competing with the traditional line-up of famous stars dressed up in their glamorous best. On both occasions Hartnell's strategy was to give the Queen a dress that was so different from theirs that she would out-dazzle them by sheer simplicity.

The first was a dramatic creation in jet-black satin with a startling white panel of satin down the front, specially woven for the Queen in Dunfermline in the pure silk satin that jockeys wore: 'I wanted to design

Typical of the matronly look which was criticised at the time as being dowdy are these two outfits (previous page and right) worn in 1949 when she was still only twenty-three. Indeterminate in outline, loose fitting, in beige or pastel colour, with the inevitable pearls and brooch, and topped with an elaborate flower-trimmed hat, they belong to the era before she found her own personal style. One concession to fashion are the ankle-straps, peep-toes and platform soles.

a very simple, tailored dress' he explained, 'for Her Majesty to wear at the Royal Film Show as a contrast to all the elaborate, fluffy dresses the stars wear'.

The 'magpie' dress created the effect he wanted, but it was so simple that it was easily copied. Three hours after the first picture appeared a copy of the dress was in a London store. Then the mass manufacturers in the rag trade got to work and the day after the first appearance of the Queen's dress mass production began, not only in black and white but also in black and pink, grey and cyclamen, wine and pink, in both satin and in velvet, as well as a bridal version in white satin and silver lamé. In a few days one hundred and twenty of the copies had been sold at £14·70, £11·55 and £9·45. Later in provincial towns copies were selling in the inexpensive dress shops for £5·25. At the end of the month paper patterns of the dress were on sale for 30p.

It is not recorded whether the Queen herself ever wore the dress again, but certainly she was never photographed wearing it, and although this brave effort to move away from the uncopiable, embroidered dresses was a failure, the second attempt was not.

This was an even simpler dress in flowing black velvet, off the shoulders, with a full sweeping skirt and no embroidery, no spangles, no trimmings whatsoever.

The Queen wore it at a Royal Film Première in 1956 with the royal emerald and diamond tiara, emerald and diamond necklace, emerald and diamond stud earrings. The rich plain black velvet, always the best background for stunning jewels and a stunning pink-and-white complexion, made a memorable impact and this time the Queen walked away with the fashion honours. (Both dresses are shown in Chapter 7.)

One other memorable black dress was the black lace gown which she wore for her Vatican visit in 1961 to meet the Pope. A long, slender slip of soft black satin is covered with black lace stiffened to stand away from the slip, and has a veil of black tulle cascading from the handsome diamond fringe tiara, so that the effect is of a slim dark figure moving in a cloud of black lace and tulle, a skilful blend of magnificence and decorum. (This dress is shown in Chapter 4.)

It took another five years before the Queen found the same sureness of touch in her day clothes, and settled for the hat and dress or coat all in one clear colour which makes her so easily distinguished in a crowd, and the simple, unfussy outline of generally tailored coat or dress with a small close-fitting turban hat or clean-cut breton which makes her (the sure mark of a personal style) recognizable anywhere, even in silhouette.

Photographed at Balmoral Castle in 1952, she wears an unspectacular suit of the kind that most of her subjects might have worn in the post-war era. Long after modern girls of her age would be 'doing their own thing' and wearing outrageous new fashions the Princess was still influenced by her parents' ideas of what she should wear, took no great interest in clothes herself, and anyway was inhibited by the drab economy. Her suit in hydrangea blue with pleated skirt is worn with sensible lace-up shoes. It is a mark of her parents' careful and modest approach in training her for her future role, that although she had been given at her wedding and was to inherit some of the most priceless jewellery in the world, she wears only her pearl necklace, her wedding and engagement rings and a sapphire brooch.

3
A Glorious Dress

The Coronation dress is the most beautiful of many beautiful dresses that the Queen has ever worn. And it is certainly the most famous modern dress in the world. Seen live on T.V., the first big royal ceremonial to be televised, millions more saw it on film, and it will live on in any history or museum of dress. The Queen's Coronation dress shimmered with a myriad soft colours like an opal and it is unlikely that anyone who saw the Queen's slow progress up the aisle of Westminster Abbey that day will ever forget that dress, so simple in outline, so light and delicate in appearance yet so intricate and heavy with symbolism. As she moved it was sometimes palest pink, sometimes pale mauve, sometimes soft green, yet the all-over effect was white.

It was Hartnell's masterpiece.

He dressed the whole Royal Family for the Coronation and the pageantry gave full scope to his particular genius. He dressed the cast, so that each was more gorgeous than the one before against a background that was already colourful and magnificent. Yet it was not only the Queen's significant role on this occasion which made her the most touchingly lovely figure of them all, it was that dress too.

The genius of theatre design began as he always did by studying the set. The Abbey was not on these occasions the cold, grey, old stone building that it sometimes seems. Lit for the ceremony by the arc lamps installed for T.V., it was bathed in brilliant gold. The carpet along the centre aisle in cerulean blue changed to pale honey as it neared the coronation area and the altar shimmered with golden plate and golden cloth. Banked each side of the carpet the peers on one side, the peeresses on the other, formed a backdrop in their robes of crimson and white.

"four-leaf shamrock for luck"

There would be a challenging clamour of colour on this occasion from the ornate copes of the clergy, from the peacock brilliance of the Indian nobility, from the splendid uniforms of pages and heralds and pursuivants, admirals and field marshals, a dazzling scene of ruby and sapphire and emerald velvet and satin, of jewels and feathers and gold. Against this background the Queen must somehow stand out, gentle but regal, solemn but gorgeous, twenty-five years old and the symbol of power.

Hartnell did his homework. He went to the London Museum and the London Library to study the history and tradition of coronation dresses, and the designs which had been made for Queen Elizabeth I, for Queen Anne and for Queen Victoria. His only brief from the Queen was that she wanted the dress to be on the same lines as her wedding dress and that it should be in white satin.

As usual, immense hard work lay behind the easy perfection of the result. He made in all nine different sketches for nine different dresses, beginning with severe simplicity and gradually becoming more ornate.

Together the Queen and he went through the suggestions. The first was for a gown rather like Queen Victoria's coronation dress, very simple in white satin with embroidery in a Greek key design round the edge of the bodice and round the hem.

The second, very slender and more modern, was embroidered in gold and edged round the hem with black and white ermine tails.

The third was a crinoline of silver tissue and white satin glittering with crystals and diamonds.

The fourth was embroidered with madonna and arum lilies and pendant pearls.

Embroidery on the Coronation dress designed for the Queen in 1952 (see pages 50 and 53). The design is a bouquet embodying the eleven emblems of Great Britain and the Commonwealth worked in delicate coloured silk thread and jewels. In the centre is the rose of England and above is the thistle of Scotland, to the right is the shamrock of Ireland and below on the left is the leek of Wales. Surrounding these are the maple leaf for Canada, the lotus flower for Ceylon, wheat, cotton and jute for Pakistan, fern for New Zealand, the wattle flower for Australia, the lotus flower for India and the protea for South Africa.

The fifth introduced colour with opal and topaz depicting wheat, amethysts for violets and rubies for roses.

The sixth was in golden, coppery colours outlining spreading branches of oak leaves and knobbly acorns dangling on crystal stalks.

The seventh had the Tudor Rose of England in gold tissue surrounded by looped fringes of golden crystal.

The eighth was in white satin embroidered in silver and crystal with all the flower emblems of Great Britain.

The Queen liked this one best and it was Hartnell's favourite too, but she thought that the white-and-silver theme might be too like her wedding gown. Hartnell recalled that Queen Victoria's Coronation gown was all white but the Queen pointed out that Victoria was a girl of eighteen and unmarried when she was crowned, while she herself was twenty-five and a married woman. She liked the idea of the flower symbols representing the United Kingdom and suggested that they should be in colour. Later she said that she wanted him to add the emblems of all the Dominions of which she was Queen.

He then drew and painted the ninth design, and the historic dress was born.

The historic and exquisite Coronation dress made for the Queen in June 1953 drawn here by Robb who, as with the wedding dress, was given a private pre-view and was able to publish this drawing on the morning of Coronation day. (A close-up view of the intricate and symbolic embroidery faces page 49). The Queen wore it later for the opening of parliaments in the Commonwealth and it is now kept at Buckingham Palace.

(opposite) Robb's drawings of the dresses made for the royal ladies at the Coronation. Each had individual embroideries on their gowns, all in the same theme of white, gold and crystal. (See page 52).

Princess Margaret

Elizabeth the Queen Mother

Maid of Honour

The Duchess of Kent

Princess Alexandra

Hartnell went to Garter King of Arms to check on the accuracy of the flowers. He tells of his horror when he was informed that it was not the daffodil, as he had thought, which was the true emblem of Wales, it was the leek. How could anyone make a lovely embroidery out of a mundane leek, could he not possibly use the graceful daffodil instead? 'No, Hartnell' said Garter sternly, 'You must have the leek'.

The next step was to make sample patterns of all the eleven emblems in pale silks lightened with crystal, pearls and opals. Palest pink for the rose of England, pale mauve for the thistle of Scotland, pale green for the shamrock of Ireland, and the despised leek looking eventually elegant in pale green with dewdrops of diamonds. Representing Canada was the maple leaf in green and gold, for Australia the wattle flower in

mimosa yellow, for New Zealand a soft green fern, for South Africa a shaded pink protea, for India a pearly lotus flower, for Pakistan wheat, cotton and jute in gold and green, for Ceylon a lotus flower in opal and mother-of-pearl.

Although the dress, covered with so much jewelled embroidery, was in fact weighty, and in order to make it hang straight and swing gracefully as she walked, it had to be lined with taffeta reinforced with horsehair, the total effect was as light as a soap bubble. It was, as the Queen said, a glorious dress.

With this dress in mind Hartnell designed dresses for the Queen Mother, Princess Margaret, the six Maids of Honour, the then Duchess of Kent, Princess Alexandra, and a couple of countesses who as Ladies of the Bedchamber would be standing nearby. The whole support-

51

ing cast were dressed in various designs of white, crystal and gold, a superb background for the Queen.

The dramatic effect of this colour scheme could not have been surpassed. As each gorgeously apparelled character entered the Abbey and took his or her appointed place, each was more breathtaking than the one before.

The procession of guests began quietly with distinguished notabilities like Lady Churchill in floating lavender chiffon (rather outshone by Sir Winston in Garter Robes with a vast pancake velvet hat topped with white ostrich feathers), the Lord Chancellor looking like the King of Spades with a coronet on top of his wig, the ambassadors and their wives, the foreign royalty, all the women in splendid gowns and glittering tiaras, the men covered with medals and gold braid. Eastern potentates joined the crowd, one in gold slashed with orange wearing emeralds and rubies, one in silver and purple tissue, followed by Queen Salote of Tonga, an imposing figure in strawberry satin. And then one by one the Royal Family entered, the Princess Royal in silver, the Duchess of Gloucester in white satin.

Finally the procession of Hartnell's ladies began. The Duchess of Kent, always elegant, in a slender white satin dress with long panels of gold embroidered up the skirt in a mosaic design, Princess Alexandra beside her in white tulle and lace lightly scattered with flowers in gold thread.

Next Princess Margaret surrounded by six Heralds who looked like a pack of cards come to life, her white satin dress more richly covered than anyone's so far, with more embroidery, more crystals, more pearls over the bodice and sweeping from hem to waist in a glittering design of marguerites and roses.

With the congregation punch-drunk by now by the mounting magnificence, there entered the Queen Mother. Glittering from top to toe she looked as if she had strolled through a field of gold. A broad band of gold tissue circled the hem and if the dress was made of satin it was not visible, for she seemed to be clothed entirely in gold and diamonds.

(opposite above) From left to right: Princess Alexandra, the Duchess of Kent, Princess Margaret, The Queen, The Queen Mother, Princess Mary and the (then) Duchess of Gloucester.

(opposite below left) The Queen with her six Maids of Honour. Left to right: Lady Moyra Hamilton, Lady Rosemary Spencer Churchill, Lady Anne Coke, Lady Jane Heathcote Drummond Willoughby, Lady Jane Vane Tempest Stuart, Lady Mary Baille Hamilton, and the Mistress of the Robes, the Dowager Duchess of Devonshire.

(opposite below right, and below) The Queen wore her Coronation dress for the opening of parliament in Wellington, New Zealand in 1954.

Leaving for Kenya on the last day of January 1952 for the tour which was cut short by the death of the King. She wears the same style of bonnet hat in draped felt which she had worn for the past few years, and a short mink jacket over her wool suit. Summoned back to England on the death of her father, black clothes had to be taken onto the aircraft so that she could walk onto British soil in mourning.

Superbly professional and (unlike her daughter who is happier when she forgets the cameras) giving the cameramen plenty of time, she slowly proceeded with a bow here to Prince Bernhard of the Netherlands, a bow there to the row of ambassadors, negotiating the tricky steps to her place with no backward glance at the trailing dress, no looking down, no hesitation, no sign of nervousness, she took her place beside the other members of the Royal Family. The congregation aflame with colour, the Royal Family seated, each wearing the Garter sash and ablaze with diamonds, the scene for the Queen's arrival is set.

Hartnell has described his anxiety as he wondered whether the dress he had made for her could possibly hold for her the centre of the stage in face of all this magnificence. But when she entered the Abbey and began her slow walk up the aisle, he must have known that he had succeeded.

Behind her were the six Maids of Honour who carried her train of imperial velvet. All six were dressed alike in white satin with trails of small golden leaves and pearl blossom; they formed a white shell for the Queen's iridescent gown.

It could not have been better done.

The Coronation was also the occasion for the most superb display of royal jewels. The Queen wore the necklace which is in many people's view her loveliest and also her simplest, a short necklet of huge single

The first formal portrait of the Queen taken since her accession shows her in the first really decollete dress she had ever worn. Designed by Hartnell in crinkled black taffeta, the bodice and skirt are shaped like big petals. With the dress she wears the diamond necklace given her as a wedding present by the Nizam of Hyderabad.

diamonds made originally for Queen Victoria from twenty-eight stones collected from a Garter Badge and ceremonial sword, with a huge single diamond as a drop on the necklet which came from the Timur ruby necklace, and single-drop diamond earrings. The Queen Mother wore this same necklet at the coronation of George VI together with another necklace of diamonds and two long strings of pearls with the Timur diamond drop inset in her crown.

It is perhaps a mark of the times that in succeeding coronations the display of jewels has grown less ostentatious. Queen Mary wore the same lovely necklet of single diamonds at King George V's coronation below eight rows of diamonds wound high round her neck, and four diamond brooches in addition to diamond bracelets and earrings.

Queen Alexandra wore the same diamond necklet for Edward VII's coronation with five rows of diamonds round her throat, an ornate looped diamond-and-pearl necklace, and a cascade of five long rows of pearls.

In contrast to the embroidered dress and the jewels and diadem which the Queen wore as she entered the Abbey was the plain white robe which she wore for the Anointing.

Queen Victoria described hers as 'a funny little shift bordered with lace'. Hartnell did better for his Queen.

Made in fine white linen, sunray pleated to fall from the neckline, it fastened at the back like a pinafore, and modestly covered, as it was symbolically designed to do, the vainglorious dress. But even here the practical demands of the situation had to be carefully considered, for the Mistress of the Robes who had to put on the white shift would be wearing long white gloves. Fiddly fastenings were therefore out of the question, modern zips notoriously tricky, and tiny buttons impossible to manipulate, so in the end large buttons with large buttonholes were chosen. On such small details can dignity and decorum depend

These behind-the-scenes details are related by Sir Norman Hartnell in his autobiography *Silver and Gold*. To the onlooker this extraordinarily beautiful royal pageant was marked by the precision of timing, the majestically organized background, the flawless dress, and the smooth performance of the chief characters in the style to which the British have become accustomed.

After the ceremony which lasted from 11 am until 2.50 pm and which required reporters to be on duty suitably dressed from 7 am until 4 pm (even women reporters were requested to wear weird little coronation head-gear), even after that stint many an experienced and toughened journalist remarked to another that the British do know how to put on a good show.

To one of them at least there remain two outstanding memories.

The slight figure of the Queen at the end of it all walking slowly down the aisle, cloaked in heavy royal crimson and ermine, a 7 lb. crown on her head, the Sceptre in one hand, the Orb in the other, and the shafts of lightning which struck across the Abbey from the two largest cut diamonds in the world, the Cullinans set in the Crown and in the Sceptre.

And that same small figure, earlier in the ceremony, giving the impression of being a little walking doll moving automatically in a clockwork pattern continually being robed and disrobed to an ancient formula, and always, wherever she moved, guarded and flanked by two solemn and magnificently dressed old men.

A charming postscript to the Coronation story expresses the hopes and the goodwill which the Queen carried with her from so many people. Hartnell on his own initiative made one little addition to the Coronation dress which he had discussed in so much detail. Unknown to her he had embroidered on the left side of the skirt one extra leaf on a shamrock to make one four-leafed shamrock for luck.

Four months after her accession the Queen visits the Scottish Crafts Centre in Edinburgh. Still in pastel colours, still in loosely draped coats, still not sufficiently interested in clothes to see that her dress and coat were the same length and still managing to overcome by her youth and charm.

"did I wear that one?"

JEWELS

The most impressive, the most famed and the most regal of the Queen's accessories are her jewels. She has at her disposal more costly jewels than any woman in the world.

Most of the costliest are Crown Jewels, not the regalia of sceptre and sword and ancient crowns, but jewels which are handed on from monarch to monarch. But the Queen has many magnificent jewels which are her personal possessions given or bequeathed to her by her grandparents or parents whose personal possession they were, or presented to her by other countries, by regiments, by private people.

But as Sir John Colville, her Private Secretary when she was Princess Elizabeth, pointed out during the controversy in 1971 about the cost of maintaining the Queen, it would be unthinkable for the Queen to sell any of them. She has an expert's eye for a good diamond. ('My best diamonds' is how she described the twenty-one diamonds given to her as a twenty-first birthday present from the Government of South Africa. Originally set in one long necklace they were later divided into a shorter necklace and a bracelet with an extra magnificent diamond presented by the De Beers Corporation set as the centre stone of the bracelet.) But she regards the jewels as a royal heritage, part and parcel of the royal job, and wears them more from a sense of duty than from any personal satisfaction that they give her. No woman who delighted in these splendid jewels for their own sake or for personal display could have burst into tears at first sight of the full rig she was expected to wear, as the Queen is reported to have done.

The most accurate and well-researched book on the subject is *The Queen's Jewellery* by Sheila Young. Among the Queen's collection the author lists 10 tiaras, 19 necklaces, 17 pairs of earrings, 13 bracelets, 34 brooches. One of these brooches incorporates the third and fourth parts of the Cullinan diamond which the Queen inherited from Queen Mary who had it made up into what is now the Queen's most valuable brooch. This priceless piece has a 62-carat square diamond from which hangs a pear-shaped diamond of 92-carats, and is lightly referred to by the Queen as 'Granny's chips'.

The Cullinan is the largest diamond ever discovered.

On her wedding, her coronation and at the death of Queen Mary the treasure chests of the royal jewels were opened for the Queen.
Seen here with the Commonwealth Premiers in December 1952 (with Winston Churchill on her immediate right), she wears the crinoline dress fashion which her mother made famous. This in mauve cotton organdie frills embroidered in white was made for her by Hardy Amies. With it she wears her first tiara and the necklace of oblong sapphires set in diamonds which was a wedding gift from her parents with matching drop earrings. Later a pendant was added, a sapphire and diamond bracelet and a sapphire and diamond tiara to complete the set.

(opposite) Dining aboard the battleship H.M.S. Vanguard in June 1953 the favourite diamond tiara is worn with the fringe diamond necklace in a Russian sunray design and diamond stud earrings. She wears pinned to the Garter sash the two royal miniatures of her father and grandfather set in diamonds. (see page 103)

Weighing about one and a half pounds, it was found near Kimberley in 1905 and named after Sir Thomas Cullinan, chairman of the Premier Diamond Company. The Transvaal Government bought the stone and Prime Minister Botha presented it to King Edward VII as a mark of friendship after the South African war, but hearing that the English settlers had voted against the gift, the King with typical diplomacy (not wishing to offend the majority who had voted for it) turned and gave the stone to his Queen.

The stone was flawed, so Asschers of Amsterdam

were commissioned to cut it into several gems, the two largest to be reserved as Crown Jewels and the rest to be the fee for cutting. King Edward bought the third largest gem for Queen Alexandra, and the remainder were bought by the South African Government and later presented to Queen Mary, so that all these became the personal property of the Royal Family.

In order of size, Cullinan One, the largest cut diamond in the world, known as 'The Star of Africa', is in the State Sceptre; Cullinan Two, the second largest cut diamond in existence is in the front of the Imperial State Crown; Three and Four form the brooch of one square diamond with a pear-shaped diamond drop which the Queen occasionally wears; Five was cut into a heart shape and set in a brooch; Six is the diamond drop on the emerald and diamond necklace which the Queen wears on the cover; Seven and Eight make the centre and pendant of another brooch; Nine was mounted by Queen Mary in a ring which the Queen seldom wears. All these are now the personal property of the Queen who on her marriage, on Queen Mary's death, and on her Coronation acquired (in addition to many other gifts of jewels) an Aladdin's Cave of the Royal Family's precious gems.

Another brooch, the world's finest rose-pink diamond was presented to her by Dr John T. Williamson, an eccentric Canadian geologist who made an immense fortune from his diamond mine in what was then called Tanganyika, a multi-millionaire who had a personal and private attachment to the Royal Family. He presented this unique diamond as an engagement present to Princess Elizabeth who had it set in the centre of a flower-spray brooch in her coronation year.

The value of the Queen's jewels is incalculable, many of the gems have been handed down through history and are irreplaceable. Pearls from Mary, Queen of Scots, diamonds from Indian princes, diamonds and pearls from Queen Victoria, diamonds from Queen Alexandra, emeralds from Queen Mary and the Timur ruby from Lahore ('It has a fascinating history' she remarks to her dresser in the B.B.C. film, 'I think we ought to get something designed specially for it').

The Queen appears to look on them as just another accessory to the job. 'Did I wear that one?' she asks her dresser handling a priceless necklace of diamonds as nonchalantly as if it were a hat, the sort of necklace that no other woman would ever forget whether she had worn or not. And, 'I think perhaps we ought to find something for the sapphires?' 'You could wear them, Ma'am, with the silver brocade' suggests the dresser.

From her ten tiaras the Queen usually selects three that she wears most often. Her favourite which she wears on grand evening occasions such as state banquets, receptions, gala performances, premières, investitures carried out in the Commonwealth countries, or formal balls, is smaller and less imposing than the others with delicate spikes each topped with a large diamond. This was her first tiara, a wedding gift from Queen Mary.

At the other end of the scale in grandeur is a diamond diadem which circles the whole head like a crown, a magnificent circlet of four bouquets of rose, shamrock and thistle and four crosses all in huge diamonds, with two rows of mammoth pearls round the band. It was made for George IV and worn by Queen Victoria, Queen Alexandra and Queen Mary. Perhaps because it is heavy the Queen wears it usually only for the State Opening of Parliament.

Her other two most usually worn tiaras are first a Russian-style tiara which is a fringe of diamonds upstanding like a sunray, which had been Queen Alexandra's wedding present from friends, and was bequeathed to Queen Elizabeth by Queen Mary. The Queen wore it for the State Openings of Parliament in Australia and New Zealand, and in Malta, and it makes an appearance on most visits to heads of state.

The other, the loveliest of them all, is a tiara of interlaced diamond circles with a huge cabochon emerald drop hanging in the centre of each circle, which can be interchanged for fifteen pearl drops.

With the emeralds she wears her fabulous emerald and diamond necklace with two drops of uneven length, one ending in a large emerald drop, the other in a diamond drop made from part of the Cullinan diamond. With the pearls she usually wears a rather heavy Victorian necklace called the Jubilee necklace (presented to Queen Victoria to celebrate her Jubilee), which has graduated pearls set in clover-leaf patterns of diamonds ending in an enormous centrepiece surmounted by a pearl and diamond crown.

Posing at Buckingham Palace for a formal photograph taken eight months after her visit to Portugal the Queen wears the same dress, as seen opposite, in white tulle finely embroidered in a shell pattern in silver and gold and diamante. This time her jewels are the superb diamond diadem edged with pearls (one of the Crown Jewels) originally made for George IV which she always wears for the State Opening of Parliament, and the necklace of diamonds and pearls was made for Queen Victoria's Jubilee in 1887.

With the plain diamond head-pieces she can choose from the magnificent sapphire and diamond necklace which was a wedding gift from her parents, with sapphire and diamond drop earrings to match, or her two necklaces of rubies and diamonds, or her aquamarines and diamonds, or one of her many, many diamond necklaces, and from an immense selection of pearl, ruby, sapphire and diamond drop or stud earrings.

While elegance is not the prime object in these displays, the daintier necklaces of huge single diamonds made like a triple or single row of beads are among the Queen's favourites.

On the cornflower-blue Garter sash which the Queen wears over her left shoulder (all other cordons except the Thistle are worn over the right shoulder) she often pins two little oval miniatures circled in diamonds, one on a pale rose-pink ribbon, the other on a pale-blue silk ribbon. These are a quaint family tradition which dates back to George IV. Known as the Royal Family Orders the present family continues the custom of wearing portraits of each other pinned to their shoulders. The Queen's two miniatures painted on ivory by Hay Wrightson and framed by Garrards, the Queen's jewellers, are of her father and grandfather, two stern, kindly and rigidly dutiful mentors for the stern, kindly, rigidly dutiful work on hand. (See page 103.)

It is a touching reminder of the woman within the finery that her only permanent jewellery from which she is never parted is a small gold watch for day time or a platinum and diamond watch in the evening which minute by minute control her hardworking day, and the comparatively inconspicuous little engagement ring.

(opposite above) The interchangeable tiara with the pearl drops again, the Jubilee necklace, the long earrings which have a large drop pearl swinging inside a frame of diamonds, and the pearl and diamond brooch, all formerly Queen Mary's. Her dress is in the palest orchid-mauve satin, the top embroidered with pearls and diamonds on orchid organza with baguette diamonds edging the waist and sleeves. This dress was made for the State visit to France in 1972 and is the one represented on the Jubilee souvenir china.

(opposite below) The same tiara here with emerald drops, an unusual emerald and diamond necklace with emerald and diamond drop earrings worn (in 1967) with a slim tailored dress by Hardy Amies of heavy gold lace over white satin.

(above) *The Queen makes an annual appearance at the Garter Ceremony at Windsor Castle where she wears the robes of the Sovereign of the Order with the Garter Chain and Star. Under the magnificent cloak of royal-blue velvet, the train held by a page of honour, the Queen wears one of the many evening dresses previously worn on tours abroad.*

(below) *Another annual appearance is at the ceremony of Trooping the Colour at the Horseguards Parade for which the Queen wears this uniform as Colonel of the Grenadier Guards and rides side-saddle. She first took over this duty as Princess when she deputised for her father who was ill, and she wore a different uniform. Here in 1956 she rides the famous old horse Winston whose regal imperturbable calm was proverbial.*

(opposite) *This formal photograph of the Queen in her Coronation regalia can only hint at its real magnificence and beauty. She wears the Imperial State Crown which is bordered with pearls and set with clusters of emeralds, sapphires and diamonds. In the centre is the Black Prince's Ruby, above it St Edward's sapphire, and below it part of the Star of Africa diamond. From the four arches hang the four pearls traditionally believed to have been Queen Elizabeth I's earrings. Her train in royal purple velvet embroidered in gold is lined with miniver. The wide gold bracelets called 'Armills' are the 'bracelets of sincerity and wisdom'. She wears the Garter Chain, but the necklace she wears here is not the one that she wore at her Coronation.*

4
State Occasions

Every state visit, and every Commonwealth tour, sets the scene for those grand resplendent dresses which Hartnell excels at designing and the Queen at wearing. State visits are visits to the head of a foreign country, the rest are visits to the Commonwealth from their own head of state, The Queen.

There are always at least two of these fabulous dresses, one for the social occasion, a banquet, a visit to the opera, a reception or a ball where the Head of State or Commonwealth is the host; and one for the return match held at the British Embassy or sometimes on the Royal Yacht where the Queen is host.

These are the occasions when the Queen puts on the style which Prince Charles is said to refer to as 'dressing up and Queening it'.

Her dress embroidered and sparkling with beads, pearls, silver, gold and diamante, the Queen may wear the Garter sash or an order of the country she is visiting, invariably wears long white gloves, and is ablaze with magnificent jewels.

The Queen can, perhaps through long familiarity with them, carry off with regal assurance more diamonds than any fashion expert would permit: diamond tiara, diamond necklace, diamond chandelier earrings, diamond bracelets, diamond brooches and diamond ring; and on her it never seems a diamond too much.

Only her rings are always modest. She wears no rings on her right hand because the endless handshaking would obviously make rings painful, and the only rings she wears on her left hand are her wedding ring and her engagement ring. This is a diamond-shaped ring with a

"dressing up and Queening it"

solitaire diamond in the centre with diamond 'shoulders', which was reset from heirloom stones belonging to Prince Philip's mother.

This diminutive figure is the star of every occasion where she appears. Sparkling from head to toe she has never looked flashy or vulgar. No matter how elegant the crowd around her, she never fails to steal the show, and not only because her diamonds are bigger and better. She has a personal royal sparkle which matches her dress and her jewels and with these three weapons she obliterates the competition.

Whenever the Queen has to plan a wardrobe for a State or Commonwealth visit there are political implications to be borne in mind, subtle compliments from one Head of State to another, courtesies which can be expressed through her clothes.

For example her grand occasion dress will often be embroidered with the national emblem of the country she is visiting, a maple leaf for Canada, wattle for Australia, cherry blossom for Japan.

Then the colour itself is important. The most famous example of the problems involved in colour alone was the celebrated occasion when the Queen Mother who was Queen at the time had a scheduled State visit to France with the King. The new dresses in lovely colours were approved and made when three weeks before she was due to depart her mother the Countess of Strathmore died, and the Court went into mourning.

The Queen realized that at such short notice the visit could hardly be cancelled. On the other hand although the French have a personal preference for black, it hardly seemed a suitable symbol for celebrating an entente cordiale.

Hartnell, summoned to the Palace to consider the problem, had a brilliant idea. He suggested that white was a royal prerogative for mourning, although purple is the colour most usually associated with royalty at these times.

It was agreed that white was the answer and Hartnell

Embroidery on the dress for the State visit to the United States in 1957 (see page 66). Flowers in pink, blue and green net are re-embroidered on sparkling 'cellophane' lace and outlined in tiny jewel beads. Bunches of grapes hanging among the flowers are outlined in colour, the centre consisting of big milky beads in pale mauve and pale green. Tiny silver and crystal embroideries give the dress lightness and delicacy.

transformed the whole collection, repeating all the dresses, silks, satins, velvet, cloth, taffeta, tulle, chiffon and lace, in white. He managed it in two weeks, the time by which the visit had been postponed.

The effect was dramatic: billowing white evening dresses made from narrow Valencienne lace threaded with silver, or thick white satin clustered with camellias. Garden-party dresses in cobweb lace and tulle worn with a hat of white ospreys or in white organdie with a white leghorn picture hat, or white crepe with a hat of white wings.

The result was so sensational that even the French, usually meagre in their praise of British clothes, were enthusiastic. Christian Dior, always more generous in his comments than his fellow designers in the Paris Haute Couture, went out of his way many years later when he was at the height of his fame to praise the

(left) The sensational dress which the Queen wore for her last night on her visit to the U.S.A. in 1957. The embroidery (detail facing page 65) of coloured net flowers appliqued to cellophane lace covered the slim-fitting dress, and the rainbow colours repeated in the tulle fantail. Hartnell reports that after a late night engagement the Queen went straight to her plane, sweeping across the tarmac in a sea of colour and sparkle, under the Klieg lights.

(opposite, left to right)
For dinner at the Chateau Frontenac in Quebec the slender dress is in lime-coloured lace re-embroidered with crystals and silver. A square train hangs from shoulders to hem.

Rome in 1961 with the Queen in an exquisite Hardy Amies dress of lace roses re-embroidered with silver thread over layers of pale blue tulle, a low back and shoe-string shoulder straps.

A dress in jade green and turquoise silk which the Queen wore at dinner aboard the royal yacht Britannia at Montreal. Her close fitting dresses looked so elegant that the line was repeated in this one gathered to outline her new slim figure and then frothing into a huge bustle.

'The Queen's slinkiest dress' was the headline in the Daily Express the day after she wore this shimmering dress, also by Hartnell, in Washington. A slender column of aquamarine blue crystals with a long matching scarf to wind round the throat and hang down the back.

white Queen. 'Whenever I try to think of something particularly beautiful' he said in a speech to guests and journalists assembled in London to see a showing of his clothes, 'I think of those lovely dresses which Mr Hartnell made for your Queen when she visited Paris.'

The colour of what the Queen wears is always a major point to be considered. On the present Queen's visit to Japan, for example, she wore an outfit in soft lilac, a simple coat with a cloche hat covered in parma violets, because lilac is the Japanese royal colour.

Then there are the jewels which have been presented to the Queen at some previous time by the people of the country she visits.

In Canada she makes a point of wearing the diamond maple-leaf brooch which the people of Canada presented to her on her eighteenth birthday; in Australia she will wear the brooch representing a spray of wattle and tritree blossoms in 150 blue and yellow diamonds which was presented to her by the Commonwealth of Australia during her State visit to Canberra in 1954. The Queen wore it the day after she received it, and remembered to wear it again when she returned to Australia nine years later.

In New Zealand in 1963 she wore the diamond fern brooch given to her on Christmas Day ten years before.

On her visit to Brazil she had a dress specially made to wear with the magnificent necklace and earrings of big square-cut aquamarines and diamonds, which took the people of Brazil a year to collect, presented to her on her Coronation. One of her favourite pieces, no doubt because it matches the colour of her eyes, she had made a small tiara of matching aquamarines and diamonds to go with it. Then the people of Brazil collected fresh

(far left) This is the lovely dress made for the Italian State visit which the Queen wore at the Scala. Beginning with lavish embroideries of deep gold and amber it shades to silver and then deepens to clustered gold round the hem. The train lined with the heavy silk of the dress is backed with the same embroidery and attached to the shoulders so that it could be swung aside when the wearer sat down. (A detail of the embroidery is on the frontispiece).

(left) The white dress embroidered with silver thread, diamonds and emerald drop beads which the Queen wore in Iran conveyed a hint (which the Queen took) that it should be worn with her diamond tiara with emerald drops. (A detail of the embroidery is on the reverse of the frontispiece).

stones and added a bracelet to match their original gift.

She wore the set when the people of Brazil saw her for the first time in 1968 – fifteen years after the gift was made – and gave her probably the most rapturous reception she has ever received.

Dozens of regimental brooches have been presented to her which she remembers to wear when she visits the regiment. At the Archers' Parade at Holyrood House in 1976 she wore the brooch given by the Archers twelve years before. The most valuable brooch in the world, which was originally cut from the Cullinan diamond, was cut in Amsterdam by the firm of Asscher in 1907. The Queen wore it in her lapel when she visited their workshop over fifty years later.

The colour she wears must also take into consideration the colour of the sash of the order of the country she visits, which she wears across the bodice of her dress on State occasions as a compliment to her hosts. Her dress must tone with the colour of the sash, not clash with it.

In Luxembourg the sash was a difficult dull orange, with which the Queen wore a dress of sea-green and gold. In England she wears the brilliant blue sash of the Order of the Garter. In France the vermilion sash of the Legion of Honour. The forethought and research which goes into this aspect of the royal clothes is seldom at fault. The sole recent mistake being a dress of emerald-green striped with green sparkling embroidery which the Queen wore in Japan – only to find that the sash she was to wear with it was a brilliant pillar-box red edged with blue. But this dress was a last-minute addition to the carefully planned wardrobe.

Not only are there these questions to be considered, but the background against which the Queen makes her appearance must be remembered, especially the vivid uniforms of the guard of honour.

For example, in France the royal arrival may be lined with the Garde Républicain dressed in

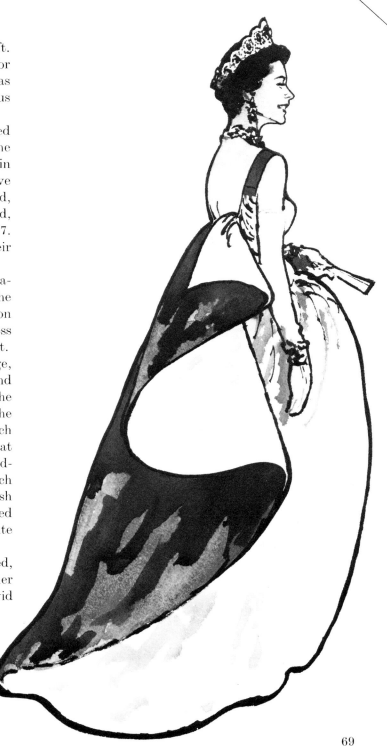

Another sensational royal dress, this time for India.
In heavy white satin with a bouffant line, the
skirt curves into a magnificent fantail lined in emerald.

69

sealing-wax red. Presented with an almost impossibly garish combination such as apple-green, violet and carrot-red uniforms in Portugal the Queen's designer usually falls back on white, or the pale green which is a background to all the flowers in the world.

And then, too, there is the decor of the palace or opera house or castle or reception rooms in which the Queen will make her first grand appearance of the visit. For this the designers will research the colours of the hangings, the upholstery, the walls, the carpets.

When the Queen visited the Versailles Opera House, this had just been redecorated in shades of blue, so for the ceremonial opening Hardy Amies (one of her three designers) made for her a dress and coat in soft grey-blue with a bodice embroidered in gold thread and crystal. When she visited the Schloss Brühl in Germany, knowing that the colours of the Bavarian Royal House were blue and white, he designed a dress with white bead embroidery on a blue background.

When she opened the Sydney Opera House in Australia Mr Amies got a friend to send over in advance patterns of the upholstery. These turned out to be in

(continued on page 78)

(top left) On one of her early Royal Tours the Queen in Nigeria (1956) visits the House of Representatives to hear a loyal address. Impervious to heat she wears a dress in heavy white satin embroidered in gold motifs and loops of gold bugles with the heavy pearl and diamond necklace, the fringe tiara, the Garter sash and star, the royal miniatures, the long white gloves and the strap-handle evening bag which together became a uniform.

(top right) On a visit to the Vienna State Opera House the Queen wears a slim white satin dress with a lattice-work design in gold.

(below left) In Yugoslavia with President Tito her dress is all gold. On gold tissue is embroidered a scallop design in bright gold beads and pear-shaped golden drops.

(below right) One of the four dresses which Hartnell made to wear under the mink-trimmed silver and white coat she wore for the 1972 visit to France (right). One in gold tissue, one in silver tissue, one in white crepe embroidered diagonally in gold and one in white satin bordered with gold.

71

(opposite and left) Embroidery on the dress for the State visit to France in 1957. On a bouffant skirt in ivory satin the emblems of France are embroidered in topaz, amber and gold. Representing the flowers of the field are poppies and marguerites, acorns and sheaves of wheat represent the harvest, and the two bees with pearly wings represent industry. Sparkling topaz, white and coffee-coloured pearls, tiny amber beads and silver sequins, and moulded golden acorn cups each with an amber pearl acorn combine to give an effect of richness and bounty.

(overleaf left) Embroidery on the dress for the State visit to Holland in 1958. Pale blue and pale pink ribbon is embroidered onto pale primrose satin with mother-of-pearl sequins in pale pink and pale blue. Scattered among these soft colours are pearly sequins in deeper blue, with sparkling jewels of aquamarine and topaz.

(overleaf right) Embroidery on the dress for the visit to Pakistan in 1961. (see page 73) On a dress of turquoise faille. White china beads are graduated to form a feather design, the centre stems embroidered in white beads and silver pailettes and crystal. The feather motifs are arranged so that they spread in separate sweeping curves over the full skirt. The sweeping bustle is in plain faille.

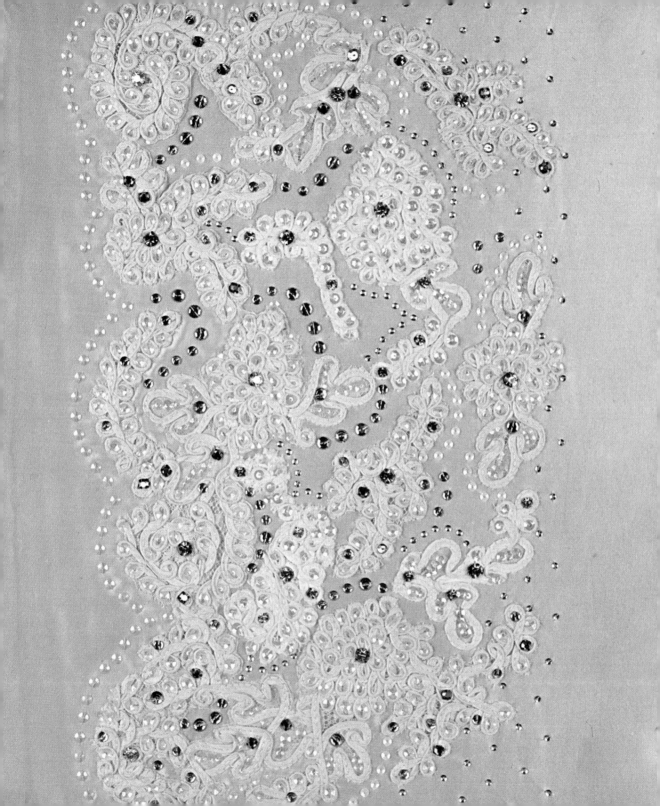

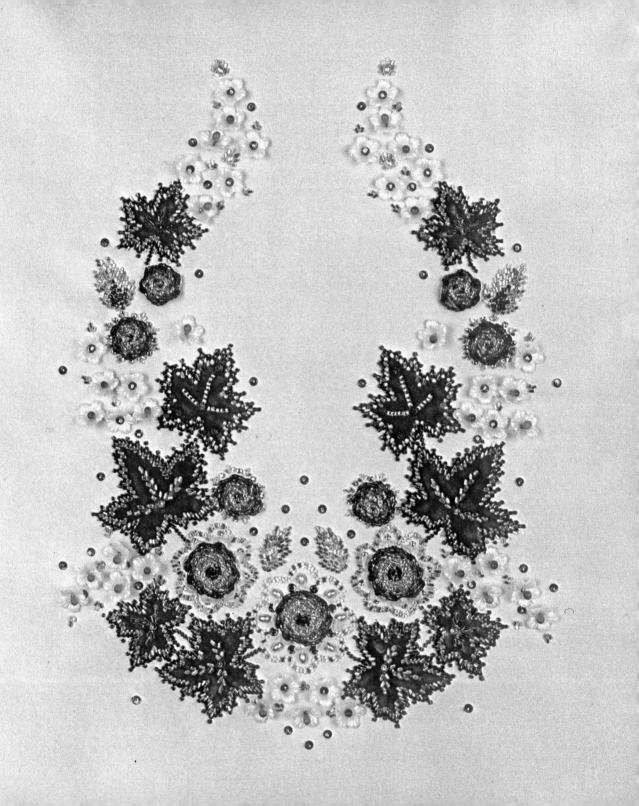

Pakistan 1961
(see caption on page 72)

(opposite and right) *For a*
banquet at Government House
in Ottawa the Queen wore her
maple leaf dress. On pale
leaf-green satin the Canadian
maple leaf emblem is ap-
pliqued in dark green velvet
edged with tiny black and
silver bugle beads. Pearly
flowers have pear-shaped
emerald centres and silver
bugle leaves, larger emerald
and silver bead flowers are
dotted among the leaves and
scattered among the flowers
and leaves in a shower of
silver beads.

73

PROGRAMME FOR THE VISIT OF HER MAJESTY THE QUEEN AND HIS ROYAL HIGHNESS THE DUKE OF EDINBURGH TO THE UNITED STATES OF AMERICA, 6–11 JULY 1976

Tuesday 6 July

10.00 am: H.M.Y. *Britannia* berths at Penn's Landing, Philadelphia.

10.30 am: The Honorable Henry Catto (Chief of Protocol of the United States) embarks H.M.Y. *Britannia* and greets The Queen and The Duke of Edinburgh.

10.35 am: Her Majesty and His Royal Highness disembark and are greeted by the Honorable Milton Shapp (Governor of Pennsylvania) and the Honorable Frank Rizzo (Mayor of Philadelphia). Dress: Lounge Suit.

10.45 am: Leave Penn's Landing by car for City Hall (*1·3 miles*).

10.55 am: Arrive City Hall.

Formally welcomed by Mayor and presented with Freedom of City, commemorative medallion and Andrew Wyeth lithographs.

11.15 am: Leave by car for Liberty Bell Pavilion (*0·8 mile*).

11.20 am: Visit Liberty Bell Pavilion.

11.30 am: Leave by car for Penn Mutual Building (*0·1 mile*). Met by Mr Charles Tyson (Chairman of the Board of the Penn Mutual Insurance Company).

11.35 am: Visit Observation Deck of Penn Mutual Building.

12 noon: Leave by car for H.M.Y. *Britannia* (*0·6 mile*).

12.05 pm: Arrive H.M.Y. *Britannia*.

12.45 pm: The Queen and The Duke of Edinburgh give a luncheon in H.M.Y. *Britannia*.

2.50 pm: Leave by car for the National Park Center Bell Tower (in the historic area) in which will hang the Bicentennial Bell, the gift of the British people to the American people (*0·5 mile*).

3·00 pm.: Arrive National Park Center Bell Tower. Received by Secretary Kleppe (Secretary of the Interior).
SPEECH: The Queen presents the Bicentennial Bell.

3.15 pm: Walk to Carpenters' Hall (*185 yards*), the Second Bank of the United States (*150 yards*) and Independence Hall (*200 yards*).

4.10 pm: Leave by car for H.M.Y. *Britannia* (*0·4 mile*).

4.15 pm: Arrive H.M.Y. *Britannia*.

4.30 pm: Receive Governors of the United States and wives.

5.30 pm: Presentation of photographs and presents in H.M.Y. *Britannia*.

6.00 pm: The Duke of Edinburgh gives a Reception on board H.M.Y. *Britannia* for American members of the Royal Society of Arts and presents to Professor Lewis the

1975 Benjamin Franklin Medal of the R.S.A.

8.15 pm: Leave H.M.Y. *Britannia* by car for the Philadelphia Art Museum (*2·8 miles*). Dress: Black Tie.

8.30 pm: Arrive Art Museum.
Received by the Mayor.
Attend a banquet given by the City of Philadelphia.

10.30 pm: Attend a Reception at the Art Museum.

Later: Return to H.M.Y. *Britannia* (*2·8 miles*).

Wednesday 7 July

8.00 am: H.M.Y. *Britannia* moves downstream to berth at Philadelphia Naval Shipyard (*7·0 miles*).

9.30 am: H.M.Y. *Britannia* berths.

10.00 am: The Queen and The Duke of Edinburgh depart from H.M.Y. *Britannia* by car for Philadelphia Airport (*5·0 miles*).

10.15 am: Depart from Philadelphia Airport by R.A.F. VC10 for Andrews Air Force Base, Washington.

11·05 am: Arrive Andrews Air Force Base and leave by car for the White House (*12 miles*). Dress: Lounge Suit.
[*Household fly by helicopter to White House*]

11·45 am: Arrive at the White House.
Greeted by the President and Mrs Ford, the Secretary of State and Mrs Kissinger, the Chairman of the Joint Chiefs of Staff and Mrs Brown, the Dean of the Diplomatic Corps, the Mayor of District of Columbia and Mrs Washington and other officials. Full military honours will be rendered.
SPEECH: Brief exchange of speeches by President Ford and The Queen.

12.15 pm: Proceed to the Blue Room for a brief Reception.

12.45 pm: The Queen and The Duke of Edinburgh lunch alone with the President and Mrs Ford.

2.30 pm: Depart by car for Arlington National Cemetery (*3 miles*).

2.40 pm: Arrive Arlington National Cemetery.

2.45 pm: Her Majesty and His Royal Highness proceed on foot and lay a wreath at the Tomb of the Unknown Soldier (*100 yards*).

3.00 pm: Leave Arlington National Cemetery by car for the Lincoln Memorial (*1·5 miles*).

3.05 pm: Visit the Memorial and adjacent areas on foot (*100 yards*).

3.30 pm: Leave by car for Blair House (*1·5 miles*).

3.35 pm: Arrive Blair House.

4.20 pm: Leave Blair House by car for the British Embassy (*2 miles*). Dress: Lounge Suit.

4.30 pm: The Queen and The Duke of Edinburgh give a Reception at the British Embassy for press, radio and television correspondents.

5.30 pm: Leave by car for Blair House (*2 miles*).

5.40 pm: Arrive Blair House.

8.00 pm: Leave by car for the White House (*100 yards*). Dress: White Tie and Decorations (Tails).

8.05 pm: Arrive White House.

SPEECH: The President and Mrs Ford give a State Dinner in honour of The Queen and The Duke of Edinburgh. The Dinner will be followed by a Reception and entertainment.

Later: Return by car to Blair House (*100 yards*).

Thursday 8 July

10.00 am: The Queen and The Duke of Edinburgh leave Blair House for the New Zealand Embassy (*2 miles*). Dress: Lounge Suit.

10.10 am: Arrive New Zealand Embassy. The Queen lays foundation stone for the new Chancery Building.

Receive Commonwealth Ambassadors. Photograph.

10.35 am: Walk through garden to the British Embassy Residence (*100 yards*).

10.40 am: Meet British Embassy staff.

Plant trees.

11.10 am: Depart British Embassy for Washington Cathedral (*1 mile*).

11.15 am: Arrive Washington Cathedral for a dedication ceremony of the Nave with the President and Mrs Ford.

11.55 am: Depart Washington Cathedral for British Embassy Residence (*1 mile*).

12 noon: Arrive British Embassy Residence and receive foreign Heads of Mission, with Commonwealth Ambassadors standing behind.

12.30 pm: Retire.

12.40 pm: Depart by car for Capitol Hill (*6 miles*).

12.55 pm: Arrive Capitol Hill.

Proceed to Rayburn Room for Reception.

1.10 pm: SPEECH. The Speaker of the House of Representatives and the Vice-President of the United States give a luncheon in honour of The Queen and The Duke of Edinburgh.

2.35 pm: Retire.

[*The Queen and The Duke of Edinburgh continue separately*]

The Queen

2.40 pm: The Queen visits the Rotunda of the Capitol Building where the Magna Carta will be on display.

2.55 pm: Leave by car for the Smithsonian Castle (*1·3 miles*).

3.00 pm: Arrive Smithsonian Castle. Received by Chief Justice Burger (Chancellor of the Smithsonian Institution), Vice-President Rockefeller (Vice-Chancellor) and the Honorable Dillon Ripley (Secretary).

Visit Smithsonian Chapel and Smithson Vault.

See Exhibition of London Treasures.

3.30 pm: Leave by car for the National Gallery (*0·75 mile*).

3.35 pm: Arrive National Gallery. Received by Mr Paul Mellon (President of the Gallery).

Visit the 'Eye of Jefferson' Exhibition (*about 400 yards*).

4.00 pm: Leave by car for the District Building (*0·75 mile*).

4.05 pm: Arrive District Building. Received by Mayor of District of Columbia and Mrs Washington.

Presentation of Key of the City.

Meet dignitaries.

4.25 pm: Leave by car for Blair House (*0·6 mile*).

4.30 pm: Arrive Blair House.

The Duke of Edinburgh

2.40 pm: Leave by car for the Washington Monument grounds (*1·75 miles*).

2.45 pm: Arrive Washington Monument and leave by helicopter for Wolf Trap, accompanied by Mrs Rockefeller (*20 miles*).

2.55 pm: Arrive Wolf Trap.

Received by Mrs Jouette Shouse (Founder of Wolf Trap Farm) and Miss Clair St Jacques (Director).

3.00 pm: Attend Matinee performance of Scottish Military Tattoo.

4.45 pm: Leave by helicopter for the Washington Monument grounds (*20 miles*).

4.55 pm: Arrive Washington Monument grounds. Proceed by car to Blair House (*0·5 mile*).

5.00 pm: Arrive Blair House.

[*The Queen and The Duke of Edinburgh continue together*]

5.30 pm: Presentation of photographs and presents.

8.10 pm: Leave by car for the British Embassy (*2 miles*). Dress: White Tie and Decorations (Tails).

8.20 pm: Arrive British Embassy.

8.25 pm: Receive President and Mrs Ford.

8.30 pm: The Queen and The Duke of Edinburgh give a Return Banquet in honour of the President of the United States and Mrs Ford.

10.15 pm: Reception in Residence grounds (1400 guests).

Later: Return by car to Blair House (*2 miles*).

Friday 9 July

9.30 am: The Queen and The Duke of Edinburgh leave Blair House by car for Andrews Air Force Base (*12 miles*). Dress: Lounge Suit.

9.50 am: Leave Andrews Air Force Base for Newark Airport, New Jersey, in R.A.F. VC10.

10.50 am: Arrive Newark Airport. Welcomed by the Honorable Brendan T. Byrne (Governor of New Jersey).

10.55 am: Depart Newark Airport by car for the Military

Ocean Terminal (U.S. Navy berth North Side) at Bayonne, accompanied by the Governor of New Jersey (*8·4 miles*).

11.10 am: Arrive Ocean Terminal, Bayonne.

Say farewell to the Governor of New Jersey and embark H.M.Y. *Britannia* for the Battery, Manhattan Island (*3·25 miles*).

H.M.Y. *Britannia* arrives off the Battery, Manhattan Island, having passed the Statue of Liberty.

12 noon: Land at the Battery by Royal Barge.

Greeted by the Honorable Hugh Carey (Governor of New York).

[H.M.Y. *Britannia will proceed afterwards to the International Passenger Terminal*]

12·05 pm: Leave by car for Federal Hall, Pine Street (*0·5 mile*).

12.15 pm: Welcomed at Federal Hall by the Honorable Abraham Beame (Mayor of the City of New York).

SPEECH: The Mayor proclaims Her Majesty an Honorary Citizen of New York and presents her with a Bicentennial Medal. Her Majesty replies.

12.35 pm: Walk along Wall Street to steps of Trinity Church. Receive Peppercorn Rent from Rector.

12.40 pm: Leave by car for Waldorf Towers Hotel (*6·4 miles*).

12·55 pm: Arrive Waldorf Towers Hotel.

Retire (35th floor).

1.20 pm: Presentation of chief luncheon guests in the West Foyer.

1.30 pm: Attend luncheon given by the Officers and Directors of the Pilgrims (Mr Hugh Bullock, President) and the English-Speaking Union (Mr John McCulloch, President).

2.40 pm: Retire.

2.50 pm: Leave Waldorf Towers Hotel by car for Morris-Jumel Mansion, West 160th Street, Edgewombe Avenue, Upper Harlem (*7·2 miles*).

3.20 pm: Arrive Morris-Jumel Mansion.

Received by Mr Percy Sutton (President, Borough of Manhattan).

3.40 pm: Leave Mansion by car for Bloomingdales (*6·2 miles*).

4.10 pm: Arrive Bloomingdales Department Store, Lexington Avenue Entrance.

Received by Mr Lawrence Lachman (Chairman of the Board).

4.35 pm: Leave Bloomingdales Department Store by Third Avenue Entrance for State Theatre, Lincoln Center (*1·8 miles*).

4.45 pm: Arrive State Theatre, Lincoln Center, for Reception given by British Societies in New York.

Received by Mr Amyas Ames (Chairman of Lincoln Center) and Mr George Robins (President of St George's Society).

5.20 pm: Leave by car for Passenger Ship Terminal to board H.M.Y. *Britannia* (*1·3 miles*).

5.25 pm: Arrive Passenger Ship Terminal.

Received by Dr William Ronan (Chairman of Port Authority). Members of staffs of British Government offices in New York will be present).

5.30 pm: Embark H.M.Y. *Britannia*.

5.45 pm: Presentation of photographs and presents.

8.30 pm: The Queen and The Duke of Edinburgh give a dinner on board H.M.Y. *Britannia*. Dress: Black Tie.

10.00 pm: Her Majesty and His Royal Highness give a Reception on board H.M.Y. *Britannia*.

Later: H.M.Y. *Britannia* sails for New Haven, Connecticut.

Saturday 10 July

10.00 am: The Queen and The Duke of Edinburgh disembark H.M.Y. *Britannia* by Royal Barge at New Haven. Dress: Lounge Suit.

10.05 am: Arrive at Long Wharf on west bank of New Haven Reach.

Received by the Honorable Ella Grasso (Governor of Connecticut) and the Honorable Frank Logue (Mayor of New Haven).

10.10 am: Leave Long Wharf for New Haven Airport accompanied by the Governor of Connecticut and the Mayor of New Haven (*6·4 miles*).

10.25 am: Arrive New Haven Airport. Say farewell to the Governor of Connecticut and the Mayor of New Haven.

10.30 am: Leave New Haven Airport by U.S.A.F. DC9 for Charlottesville, Virginia.

11.35 am: Arrive Charlottesville Airport.

Greeted by the Honorable Mills Godwin (Governor of Virginia).

Leave by car for University of Virginia accompanied by the Governor of Virginia (*9 miles*).

12 noon: Arrive The Lawn, University of Virginia.

Received by Dr Frank Hereford (President, University of Virginia), the Mayor of Charlottesville and other state and civic dignitaries.

12.05 pm: On the steps of Cabell House, Her Majesty hands to the Governor of Virginia a devisal of the Arms used by the Virginia Company of London and later by the Royal Colony and Dominion of Virginia.

12.15 pm: Walk up Lawn through guests.

Visit a student's room.

12.35 pm: Retire in Pavilion.

12.45 pm: Luncheon in the Rotunda given by Governor.

2.00 pm: Retire in Pavilion.
2.15 pm: Leave University of Virginia by car for Western Virginia Bicentennial Center (*4·4 miles*).
2.30 pm: Arrive Western Virginia Bicentennial Center. Received by Mr Lewis McMurran (Chairman).
2.50 pm: Leave by car for Monticello (*3 miles*).
3.00 pm: Arrive Monticello. Received by Mr Frederick Notting (Chairman of Thomas Jefferson Memorial Foundation).
3.35 pm: Leave Monticello by car for Charlottesville Airport (*17·8 miles*).
4.05 pm: Depart from Charlottesville Airport in U.S.A.F. DC9 for Providence, Rhode Island.
5.15 pm: Arrive Providence, Rhode Island.
Greeted by the Honorable Philip Noel (Governor of Rhode Island) and the Honorable Vincent A. Ciancia (Mayor of Providence).
5.20 pm: Depart Airport by car for Newport (*28·6 miles*).
5.50 pm: Cross Newport Bridge into Newport.
5.55 pm: Arrive Queen Anne Square. Received by the Honorable Humphrey Donnelly (Mayor of Newport).
Open Square and walk through Trinity Church to cars.
6.10 pm: Proceed to U.S. Navy Base.
6.20 pm: Arrive U.S. Navy Base. Received by Mr Robert Silva (President of the Council of Middletown).
Embark H.M.Y. *Britannia*.
8.30 pm: The Queen and The Duke of Edinburgh give a dinner on H.M.Y. *Britannia* in honour of the President and Mrs Ford. Dress: Black Tie.
Later: H.M.Y. *Britannia* sails for Boston.

Sunday 11 July
9.30 am: H.M.Y. *Britannia* enters Boston harbour and is greeted by a 21-gun salute from U.S.S. *Constitution*. Dress: Lounge Suit.
10.00 am: H.M.Y. *Britannia* berths at Coast Guard Base.
10.30 am: The Queen and The Duke of Edinburgh disembark from H.M.Y. *Britannia*.
Greeted by the Honorable Michael S. Dukakis (Governor of Massachusetts) and the Honorable Kevin White (Mayor of Boston).
10.40 am: Proceed by car to the Old North Church (*0·5 mile*).
10.45 am: Attend morning service at the Old North Church. Greeted by the Reverend R. Golledge (Vicar).
The Duke of Edinburgh reads second lesson.
11.45 am: Proceed by car from Old North Church, Unity Street, to the Old State House, passing Paul Revere's house. (*0·75 mile*).

12 noon: Arrive Old State House.
Greeted by Mr W. Osgood (President of the Bostonian Society).
Tour of Old State House.
The Queen and The Duke of Edinburgh appear on the balcony.
Proceed outside to platform.
12.20 pm: Poem recital by Mr D. McCord and historical oration by Mr W. Whitehill.
SPEECH: The Queen replies.
12.30 pm: Proceed on foot to City Hall for luncheon given by the Mayor (*300 yards*).
12.40 pm: Arrive Mayor's suite.
Retire.
12.50 pm: Pre-lunch drinks.
1.05 pm: Lunch given by the Mayor.
2.30 pm: Retire.
2.40 pm: Depart City Hall on foot past ethnic groups performing in Square.
2.55 pm: Arrive Reviewing Stand in front of Fanueil Hall. Received by Mr Elliot Richardson (Secretary of Commerce). Parade of Ancient and Honorable Artillery Company and other units.
3.15 pm: Presentation of gift of spoons.
3.20 pm: Depart Reviewing Stand for drive through Boston.
3.50 pm: Arrive U.S.S. *Constitution*.
Received by the Honorable J. W. Middendorf (Secretary of the Navy).
4.10 pm: Depart U.S.S. *Constitution* on foot for H.M.Y. *Britannia*.
4.15 pm: Arrive H.M.Y. *Britannia*.
4.30 pm: Presentation of photographs and presents.
6.00 pm: The Queen and The Duke of Edinburgh give a Reception on board H.M.Y. *Britannia*.
7.30 pm: H.M.Y. *Britannia* sails from Boston for Halifax, Nova Scotia.

shades of purple, red, orange and maize – a sizeable competition for any dress. Mr Amies designed a dress in three shades of flame coloured net with an embroidered top and cape which succeeded in making the colours in the house recede to their proper place as a background.

More than this, a different state dress must be designed for each separate occasion in the same country. If the Queen wore a magnificent dress of yellow and gold in Ottawa, she would not appear even for an exactly similar occasion in the same dress in Montreal. The people of Montreal might consider it an affront to them if, for the Queen's grandest gala welcome in their town, she wore the dress which they had already seen in their morning papers.

Add to all these problems that somehow, in a kaleidoscope of immense crowds excitedly waving handkerchiefs and flags, this one figure must be seen and easily picked out. In Rio she wore the same vivid purples and greens as the dancers, the local prints associated with the country, strong emeralds and shocking pink which suited the strong sunshine. But in general she now relies on an all-in-one-colour plain outfit which singles her out, a formula most successfully carried out when, at the opening of the Olympics in Montreal, the one clearly visible figure among that crowd of 78,000 and to the millions watching on T.V. was the figure dressed in brilliant cyclamen.

Nor is this all. When Her Majesty appears in a group with the other royals no two must appear in the same colour, no two must clash, no two must wear the same sort of hat. And the Queen must always command the stage.

Hartnell, whose long training in the theatre designing for most of our famous actresses in the days of flamboyance and elegance – Alice Delysia, Mistinguett, Gertrude Lawrence, Isabel Jeans – for Noel Coward plays and for Cochrane musicals, is experienced in the skills of dressing the cast, and knowing how to give the principal the best entrance. He knows how to make a dramatic effect, whether it be with plain white or on occasions with plain black, and better than anyone he knows how to build up the cast in a crescendo so that as each personage enters, each is more eyecatching than the one before until the breathtaking arrival of the star herself.

One final point which is not generally realized about the Queen's clothes is the sheer practical common sense which dictates so much of what she wears.

On State occasions there must always be a shoulder strap or top to the bodice which allows the Garter or other sash to be pinned to her shoulder, and the two miniatures which she so often wears pinned just below her shoulder. The dress must never have a long train lest some flustered diplomat should tread on it and be embarrassed. Hem lengths must always be toe-free to allow the Queen to walk without lifting her skirt or catching her heel or foot in the hem.

Day clothes must be easy to walk in and to sit in. They must never be so short that they reveal too much leg when she sits, usually on a platform raised above the heads of the crowd. Neither must they be too full so that a wind may lift them above the brink of decorum. More than that they must be easily packed and easily pressed, since often the pressing must be done on the royal train. Jersey fabric must never be used because it is too clinging and the hems tend to droop. Fastenings must be simple and easy, no tiny buttons for example, for the Queen may have to change four times a day. Coats, unless they are of the kind that are part of the dress, are a troublesome extra and pose the problem of the inelegant posture involved in getting out of them. Extra scarves, cloaks or wraps present a problem. ('What should I do with it?', the Queen reasonably asks) except on occasions where she has a retiring room.

Moreover, for all public and state occasions evening dresses must be cut low enough to show off the magnificent royal necklaces of sapphires, emeralds, rubies and diamonds which hang not at the fashionable length of choker necklets or waist-length strings, but are a medium length. Although the Queen has over the years removed a pendant or used part of a stomacher as a brooch, she obviously cannot alter the royal jewels with every passing fashion.

*Germany 1965
(see caption overleaf)*

Vatican 1961 (see caption overleaf)

(*opposite above left*) *Lace used for the dress the Queen wore on her visit to the Vatican in 1961 (see previous page). Mounted on stiff net so that it formed a bell-shaped skirt over a slim black slip, flowers cut from the lace were appliquéd round the black net yoke and edged the black tulle veil.*

(*opposite above right*) *Embroidery on the dress for the State visit to Germany in 1965 (see previous page). Fine cobweb lace over silver lamé is re-embroidered in a design which follows the scalloped design of the lace in white china beads, mother-of-pearl sequins and diamanté.*

(*opposite below left*) *Embroidery on an evening coat for the State visit to France in 1967. In complete contrast to the lavish and richly jewelled fabrics is this delicate white lace over heavy dull silk re-embroidered in palest pink and silver pearls and opalescent sequins sprinkled with dewdrops of diamond.*

(*opposite below right*) *Embroidery on the dress for the Royal visit to Australia in 1974 (see Robb drawing on this page). On a dress of pale green and mimosa-yellow net over satin are embroidered the wattle flowers of Australia. Soft tufts of yellow mimosa have leaves edged in gold bugle beads with stems of pearls and smaller leaves of curved gold with pearls cupped along the centre.*

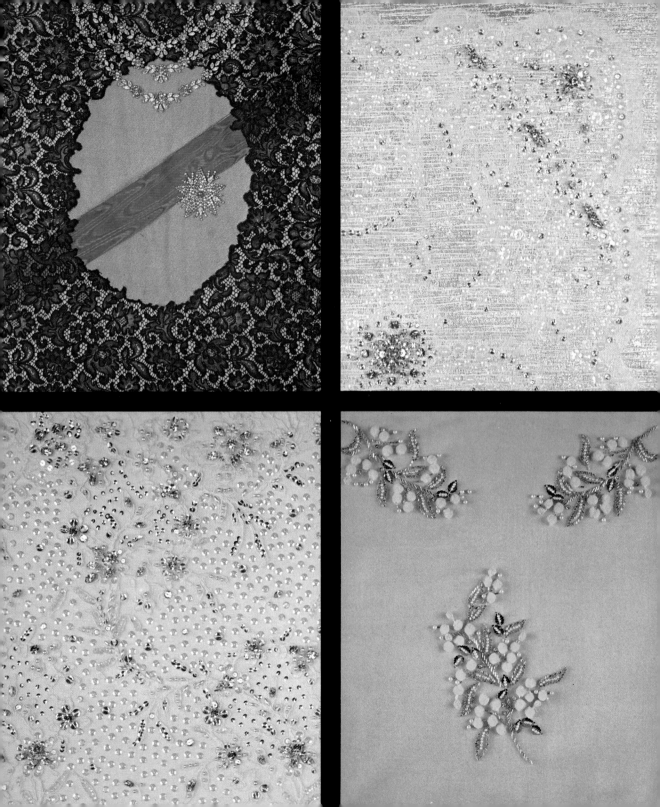

5
Worldwide Travel

It is in her vast social round which circumscribes the globe that the special demands which distinguish the Queen's clothes from that of any other woman are most marked. From 1952, when she became Queen, until 1975 she had in foreign tours alone travelled the equivalent of seventeen times round the world. And this does not include the trips made when she was Princess Elizabeth, nor the visits to Finland and to the U.S.A., to Bermuda and Canada in 1976. Nor does it include the unending cycle of tours around Britain.

Each year there lies ahead of her an immense schedule of appointments. No one can assess the number of schools, factories and hospitals, the regiments and guards of honour which she has inspected, the number of royal and civic addresses she has listened to in towns and capitals all over the world, the number of trees she has planted and foundation stones she has laid, the hands she has shaken, the medals and regimental colours she has presented, the opening ceremonies she has performed, the luncheons, dinners and receptions she has given and attended, the investitures and audiences she has held, or the displays of dancing she has watched: from schoolchildren in Huddersfield and Pudsey to Maori dancing in Rotorua, New Zealand. 'All those children!', she remarked after her first Canadian tour when she was Princess Elizabeth, 'I wonder how many I have seen? I think we must have met every child in Canada'.

An unusual dress in an unusual colour worn for an investiture in Nigeria in 1956, which shows off the Queen's slim waist. In dark green silk taffeta the true colour of a good emerald, woven with ribbons of gold, the skirt is gathered into the waist and opens over a panel of plain taffeta bordered round the hem with a deep band of gold and green. The jewels are the Russian fringe diamond tiara, diamond single-drop earrings, and the necklet of single diamonds with a diamond drop is the one which she wore at her Coronation. Across her dress she wears the Garter Sash and Star.

"what a hurry she is in"

Nor can anyone estimate the number of clothes she has worn.

In the B.B.C. film on 'The Royal Family' they estimated that she holds in this country 13 investitures a year involving 2000 people, and this does not count the knights she has dubbed in the Commonwealth; that in the tour of Brazil and Chile she made 12 separate journeys by air and 79 by road; that she has attended 21 different evening receptions in 23 days; that in one diplomatic evening held at Buckingham Palace she greeted 1400 guests from 107 different countries; that in the four palace garden parties held each year she has over 8000 guests at each, a year's total of over 30,000 people.

It is not unusual to give receptions for 1500 people which means that although each guest shakes hands with the Queen once, the Queen shakes hands 1500 times in one evening. She can have as many as nine different engagements in one day, usually three, sometimes four changes of dress. On her 1976 State Visit to the U.S.A. a typical day began with her first public appearance at 10 am and continued until midnight with two ten-minute breaks, one before and one after luncheon, and a two to two-and-a-half hour break between about 6 and 8 pm when she could rest and change for the evening round. And this pace was kept up for six days without let-up, in July, in a heat wave.

It is anyone's guess how many clothes this would involve. But in their book *The Queen's Life* Graham and Heather Fisher estimate that for her short tour to Japan she took thirty dresses specially made for the visit, although of course these were worn for other occasions later.

Equally admirable is the organization behind the travels which enables the Queen to sail through this crowded schedule impeccably turned out in clothes which never distract her from the work in hand.

She must plan clothes which are suitable for travelling by train, plane, car, horse and carriage, yacht and tender, by elephant in India, and in a splendid golden

(left) In Waitangi, New Zealand on one of her early tours, a year after she was crowned, the Queen wears one of the light summer prints, fairly full-skirted, fairly long, with loosely draped bodice which she favoured before she found her own style.

In Nigeria in February 1956 (centre) in emerald and white print dress; red and pink print in Sweden in June of the same year (right). The Queen still favours the fichu neck-lines and full skirts.

chariot drawn by forty men in Borneo. She must plan for unrelenting heat or intense cold, pouring rain, for muggy humid atmosphere, for cold high wind. The clothes must cover a wide range, suitable for a mayoral luncheon in a grey north of England town and for carrying the British flag into cities as flamboyant as Rio de Janeiro.

She is careful, within the context of her position, to make such economies as are consistent with her special role. They are not sensational but they do refute any charge of personal extravagance. Nothing causes more resentment among those who work for her than the

legend that when she has finished wearing her clothes they are ripped up. On the contrary, they are worn again and again, often for several years, and a favourite dress may be worn into the ground. Added to this, they are rained on, sat on, cleaned, re-cleaned, packed, unpacked, pressed, lengthened, shortened and laundered. Buckingham Palace do not feel it tactful to reveal the ultimate fate of royal clothes.

However, it is no secret that her two most famous ceremonial dresses are kept at the Palace.

Her wedding dress has twice been lent out for display in aid of the Church of England's Children's Society, once in Badminton in 1969 and once in Sudeley Castle, Gloucestershire, in 1970, and it was also lent for display in the London Museum in 1972 and 1973.

The Coronation dress was worn at a grand reception at Buckingham Palace and also at a reception during Coronation celebrations in Scotland at Holyrood House in 1953. In 1953 and 1954 she took it on her visit to New Zealand, Australia and Ceylon and wore it for the ceremonial openings of parliament in Wellington,

Canberra and Colombo. (She also opened four state parliaments in Australia which involved four separate grand dresses). She wore the Coronation dress again in Canada to open parliament in Ottawa in 1957, and in 1966 the dress was lent for display at the Westminster Abbey Treasure Exhibition in connection with the Abbey's celebration of its 900th anniversary.

As for the other clothes, there are many examples of their being worn many times over. For example, Hartnell's grand silver tissue coat edged with white mink made for the Paris trip in July 1972 was worn for the Opening of Parliament at Westminster in November 1976. The brown-and-white Hardy Amies outfit which she wore for her arrival in Paris turned up at Ascot later that year. The pink-and-white check coat over a pink dress made by Ian Thomas, her new designer, which she wore for her Tokyo State Visit in May 1975 was still much in evidence in November 1976.

It would be considered lacking in diplomacy if she took on official visits abroad the same clothes that she had been seen wearing earlier in Britain, but for social occasions like Ascot and other race meetings where there are no official toes to tread on, she can wear the same outfits that have been much photographed abroad; and there are in addition the investitures and audiences and dinner parties at Buckingham Palace where she is not photographed and where the same clothes will be made to earn their cost.

Hats and coats and dresses are made interchangeable. There will generally be two or three dresses to wear with the same coat, two or three hats to go with each outfit. There are three grand dresses in gold and silver to wear under the silver and mink coat; a white silk or linen coat can be worn over almost any print which has a white background.

For her arrival in Tokyo when she wore the lilac coat and lilac hat over a green printed dress she changed into a hat which matched the dress when she wore it without the coat. And several of her hats have interchangeable trimmings which match several different dresses.

Although her clothes are sometimes outdated by a new switch in fashion because she has to plan so far in advance (a recent example was the sudden advent of the new longer skirt which made her skirt length seem a little too short to the fashion-conscious and fashion-trade-dominated Americans in 1976), the Queen would never order a new set of clothes on this account. Not only because she is not over-bothered by fashion and makes what use she wants out of it – having discovered what suits her and her job she stays with it – but also because she would never countenance an expense which would make her seem indifferent to the economic situation of her country. It is on record that she likes to know in advance what a dress will cost and with the staggering rise in the cost of materials and difficulty in getting

The brown-and-white outfit worn in Paris in 1972 turned up later that year when she drove down the course at Ascot with the Shah of Persia. An unusual choice for the Queen who generally avoids dark colours, it was a great success with the French press.

them, her designers sometimes feel obliged to warn her of this in advance.

The royal programme for the Queen's U.S.A. state visit (see pages 74–77) gives some idea of the organization that is required in respect of clothes alone.

To maintain the precise timing for which the Royal Family is famous the diary of events is first settled in principle with Her Majesty, and then her Private Secretary does a reconnaissance of the route and times the various distances, engagements, length of speeches and so on. Not much time is left over for the Queen to change her dresses and she has become one of the speediest dressers on record.

Two photographs which indicate the strain imposed by these exhausting tours. Leaving London airport for Canada in the first week of July 1970 in a trim white coat and breton hat, she returns to London airport eleven gruelling days later for once unable to conceal her obvious tiredness.

'You cannot imagine' said one of the entourage, 'what a hurry the Queen is sometimes in'. She can put on her hat without looking, and her tiara while running downstairs, yet they are never awry. The fastenings on everything she wears must be sure and quick. Her hair after wearing and removing a couple of hats must still be shining and groomed for the evening tiara. Her make-up must stay immaculate through a heat-wave from ten in the morning until her first ten-minute respite at around 12.30. The Queen is almost never seen to renew her lipstick in public, and probably because she wears only a light make-up, has a beautiful skin, and seems impervious to heat, more frequent repairs are not necessary.

In the interests of speed and immaculate results the Queen has with her on foreign trips two dressers and a hairdresser always in attendance.

The pressing which is essential before the Queen wears her clothes may have to be done on the royal train or in the royal plane. The details of the outfit, the accessories, hats, shoes, bags and gloves, must always be prepared in advance, a task in which Miss Margaret Macdonald, the Queen's head dresser, is helped by the designer's original sketches (in one case presented in a little book) with fabric patterns attached, and by the milliners who attach patterns of the dress with which the hat is to be worn pinned to each hat.

Nor must it be forgotten that the Queen must take with her the special order which has been previously presented to her by the head of state whom she is visiting, such as the orange sash with blue selvedge of the Order of the Golden Lion of the House of Nassau presented by the Grand Duke and Duchess of Luxembourg which she must wear in Luxembourg, or the bright red cordon edged with dark purple-blue of the Supreme Order of the Chrysanthemum, previously presented by the Crown Prince and Princess of Japan, when she goes to Tokyo.

The Queen's luggage when she goes on a prolonged royal tour is mountainous, for it may contain presents for the heads of state as well as on some occasions

(continued on page 88)

In Malaysia in February 1972 she wears for her arrival a dress of slub silk in two shades of mignonette green with a hat to match. The darker shade is in the band round the hem and round her hat.

In Philadelphia in 1976 in one of her most successful outfits by Hardy Amies. The dress in navy-blue and white chiffon under a crepe-de-chine coat in the same navy and white stripes is worn with a wide-brimmed hat in white-stitched organza trimmed with a navy petersham band.

OVERSEAS VISITS BY THE QUEEN WHEN SOVEREIGN (Accompanied by The Duke of Edinburgh unless marked*)

1952
Kenya: 6 February

1953
Canada (refuelling stop): 24 November
Bermuda: 24–25 November
Jamaica: 25–27 November
Panama: 29 November
Fiji: 17–19 December
Tonga: 19–20 December
New Zealand: 23 December–30 January 1954

1954
Australia: 3 February–1 April
Cocos Islands: 5 April

Ceylon: 10–21 April
Aden: 27 April
Uganda: 28–30 April
Libya: 1 May
Malta: 3–7 May
Gibraltar: 10 May
Total distance: 43,618 miles (24 November 1953–10 May 1954)

1955
Norway (State Visit): 24–26 June

1956
Nigeria: 28 January–16 February
Total distance: 8,958 miles
Corsica, Sardinia (private cruise in H.M.Y. *Britannia*): 10–18 March
Sweden (State Visit): 8–17 June

1957
Portugal (State Visit): 16–21 February
France (State Visit): 8–11 April
Denmark (State Visit): 21–25 May
Canada: 12–16 October
U.S.A. (State Visit): 16–21 October

1958
Netherlands (State Visit): 25–27 March

1959
Canada: 18 June–5 July
U.S.A.: 6 July
Canada: 7 July–1 August
Total distance: 17,633 miles

1960
Denmark: 21–25 October

1961
Cyprus (refuelling stop): 20 January
India: 21 January–1 February

Pakistan: 1–16 February
India: 16–26 February
Nepal (State Visit): 26 February–1 March
India: 1–2 March
Iran (State Visit): 2–6 March
Turkey (refuelling stop): 6 March
Total distance: 21,402 miles
Italy (private): 29 April–1 May
Italy (State Visit): 2–5 May
Italy (Vatican City State Visit): 5 May
Italy: 5–9 May
Ghana: 9–20 November
Liberia (State Visit): 23 November
Sierra Leone: 25 November–1 December
Gambia: 3–5 December
Senegal* (refuelling stop): 6 December
Total distance: 9,189 miles

1962
Netherlands: 1–3 May

1963
Canada (refuelling and overnight stop): 31 January–1 February
Hawaii (refuelling stop): 1 February
Fiji: 2–3 February
New Zealand: 6–18 February
Australia: 18 February–27 March
Fiji (refuelling stop): 28 March
Hawaii (refuelling stop): 29 March
Canada: 29 March
Total distance: 42,062 miles

1964
Canada: 5–13 October
Total distance: 7,551 miles

1965
Ethiopia (State Visit): 1–8 February

Back from her tour again in July 1976 the Queen wears a coat and dress made for her tour to Japan. In strong turquoise patterned with white the coat is in crepe-de-chine, the dress in a matching print is in chiffon, and hat brim is faced in the same material as the coat. And once again she shows unmistakeable signs of the toll which these tours exact.

Sudan (State Visit): 8–12 February
Total distance: 9,735 miles
Germany (State Visit): 18–28 May
Total distance: 3,078 miles

1966
Canada (refuelling stop): 1 February
Barbados: 1 February
Mustique (private): 2 February
British Guiana: 4–5 February
Trinidad: 7–9 February
Tobago: 10 February
Grenada: 11 February
St Vincent: 13 February
Barbados: 14–15 February
St Lucia: 16 February
Antigua (private): 17 February
Dominica: 18 February
Montserrat: 19 February
Antigua: 20 February
Antigua (private): 21 February
St Kitts: 22 February
Nevis: 22 February
British Virgin Islands: 23 February
Turks and Caicos Islands: 25 February
Conception Island (private): 26
  February
The Bahamas: 27–28 February
Conception Island (private): 1 March
Jamaica: 3–6 March
U.S.A.* (refuelling stop): 7 March
Total distance: 15,527 miles
Belgium (State Visit): 9–13 May

1967
France* (private): 26–29 May
Canada: 29 June–5 July
Total distance: 7,156 miles
Germany*: 14 July
Malta: 14–17 November
Total distance: 2,909 miles

1968
Senegal* (refuelling stop): 1 November
Brazil (State Visit): 1–11 November
Chile (State Visit): 11–18 November
Brazil: 18–19 November
Senegal (refuelling stop): 19 November
Total distance: 18,900 miles

1969
Austria (State Visit): 5–10 May
Norway: 7–12 August

1970
Canada (refuelling and overnight
  stop): 2–3 March
Hawaii (refuelling stop): 3 March
Fiji: 4–5 March
Tonga: 7 March
New Zealand: 12–30 March
Australia: 30 March–3 May
Fiji (refuelling stop): 3 May
Hawaii: 3 May
Canada (refuelling stop): 3–4 May
Total distance: 39,872 miles
Canada: 5–15 July
Total distance: 12,350 miles

1971
Canada: 3–12 May
Total distance: 13,532 miles
Turkey (State Visit): 18–25 October

1972
Bahrain (refuelling stop): 8 February
Thailand (State Visit): 9–15 February
Singapore: 18–20 February
Malaysia: 22–26, 28 February
Brunei: 29 February
Malaysia: 2 March
Singapore: 5 March
Malaysia: 6, 8 March
Maldives (State Visit): 13–15 March
Seychelles: 19–20 March
Mauritius: 24–26 March
Kenya: 26 March
Total distance: 24,000 miles
France (State Visit): 15–19 May
Yugoslavia (State Visit): 17–21 October

1973
Canada: 25 June–5 July
Total distance: 10,000 miles
Canada: 31 July–4 August
Total distance: 6,700 miles
Canada* (refuelling stop): 15 October
Hawaii* (refuelling stop): 15 October
Fiji* (overnight stop): 16–17 October

Australia: 17–22 October
Singapore* (refuelling stop): 23
  October
Iran* (refuelling stop): 23 October
Total distance: 24,100 miles

1974
Canada* (refuelling stop): 27 January
Hawaii* (refuelling stop): 28 January
Cook Islands*: 28–29 January
New Zealand: 30 January–8 February
Norfolk Island: 11 February
New Hebrides: 15–16 February
British Solomon Islands: 18–
  21 February
Papua New Guinea: 22–27 February
Australia: 27–28 February
Singapore* (refuelling stop): 28
  February
Dubai* (refuelling stop): 1 March
Dubai* (refuelling stop): 14 March
Singapore*: 14 March
Indonesia (State Visit): 14–22 March
Singapore (refuelling stop): 22 March
Dubai (refuelling stop): 23 March
Total distance: 55,000 miles
France* (private): 16 June

1975
Bermuda: 16–18 February
Barbados: 18–20 February
The Bahamas: 20–21 February
Mexico: 24 February–1 March
Bermuda (refuelling stop): 1 March
Total distance: 16,032 miles
Jamaica: 26–30 April
U.S.A. (refuelling stop): 1 May
Hawaii: 1–3 May
Guam (refuelling stop): 4 May
Hong Kong: 4–7 May
Japan (State Visit): 7–12 May
U.S.A. (refuelling stop): 12 May
Total distance: 26,300 miles

1976
Finland (State Visit): 24–28 May
Bermuda: 3 July
U.S.A. (State Visit): 6–11 July
Canada: 13–24 July

special plate for the reception at the Embassy. And in addition there will be hat boxes, shoe boxes, wardrobe trunks, the grand gala dress to be packed, the priceless jewels and tiaras in a separate case.

Someone once estimated that she took as much as six tons of luggage for her visit to Mexico, but as the Palace point out no one has ever weighed it, and possibly even this does not equal the weight of luggage carried around by the Duke of Wellington in his campaign.

What is known is the motley collection of trunks, cases, even zip bags which pile up outside the Palace before she leaves (and often well in advance since they must arrive at their destination before she does). There is no suite of elegantly matched luggage but far more distinguished is the simple address in large letters on each side of every piece which says 'The Queen'.

(opposite) One of the new softer styles which made all the clothes designed for her U.S.A. trip in 1976 so widely praised. This one, by Hartnell, which she wore in Washington, is in a delicate wisteria-mauve and white printed chiffon with a gently flared skirt and a cape which is attached to the front of the bodice and covers her arms. The hat, in a matching pale mauve straw swathed with the same material, manages to be wide brimmed and still sufficiently off the face to meet the royal rule that the Queen's face must not be hidden. White accessories pick up the white in the print, and in addition to the triple row of pearls and pearl stud earrings she wears the beautiful brooch of a large pearl circled with three rows of diamonds with three large drop pearls.

(overleaf left) Embroidery for the State visit to Japan in 1975 (see page 110, bottom left). On pale blue chiffon are sewn clusters of cherry-blossom in pale pink. Each flower has petals of palest pink organdie with a centre of pink pearl and crystal stamens or in deeper pink sequins. The small leaves are in mother-of-pearl and the background sparkles with a shower of tiny silver and pink sequins.

(overleaf right) Embroidery for the dress for the State visit to Japan in 1975 (see Robb drawing on this page). Scalloped fringes of pale gold are embroidered on a dress of thick white taffeta. On the scalloped bands are flowers of topaz, amber pearls and gold pailettes with alternating lilies in gold which have stamens in gold thread and pearl. From this band hangs the scalloped fringes of pale golden bugles.

6
Regal Accessories

The problem (in fashion terms) of what to wear with what is one which is easily solved in the case of the Queen. Excepting only her hats, it is primarily the practical aspect which decides the style more than demands of fashion or elegance.

The Queen is on her feet more than the most hardworked nurse. She stands and walks at the garden parties, she walks to inspect factories and schools and housing estates and hospitals, she walks up and down the rows of guards lined up for her inspection, she stands to receive ambassadors, to confer knighthoods and to award honours, she stands at receptions and to greet the guests. At one afternoon reception at the British Embassy in Washington she shook hands with 1574 guests standing for one hour and fifty minutes with only one five-minute break for a cup of tea. She stands to deliver speeches, exchange gifts, look at art museums and exhibitions, to lay wreaths. And she stands for her dress fittings.

This sort of pace goes on week after week, year after year, with a stamina which, like Queen Mary's, exhausts many of her younger entourage. 'When I was a child' the Queen says, 'my grandmother used to tell me that I would have to stand a lot all my life. I'm accustomed to it and I don't mind'.

The extent to which her work depends on footwork means that her shoes must above all be comfortable. The Australian press which once asked sharply: 'Does the Queen possess only one pair of shoes?' cannot have fully appreciated the connection between comfortable

"my grandmother told me"

and well-fitting shoes and a carefree smile.

Like most girls she sacrificed comfort to fashion when she was younger and wore the platform soles, ankle straps, and peep toes which were current at the time. But she never followed the fashion for pointed toes and stiletto heels which was not only extremely uncomfortable but dangerously unbalanced and difficult to walk in. She never wears the pale glove-suede shoes which can be ruined in one shower of rain, she never wears the paper-thin soles which make the pavements feel red-hot, and she never wears the delicate evening shoes which are no more than a sole and thin criss-cross of straps.

There is not only the interminable standing and walking to be considered: she must also be able to negotiate a gangplank from ship to shore, which has even involved a leap in choppy seas from the royal barge to the royal landing place. She must be able to step with lighthearted assurance down from an airplane or up a ship's ladder to greet the waiting crowds, she must be able to climb into a coach with high and rickety tail-boards, or even on one occasion into the driver's cab of a train. In long evening dress with a diadem on her head she must be able to walk up or down long flights of steps without looking down, for a Queen on a stately occasion with a diadem on her head must keep her head regally in the air. And she must be able to do all this in fair weather and foul and never once slip, trip, turn her ankle or falter.

Walkabouts, before they became an exercise in public relations, were always an integral part of her work.

Her shoes are therefore generally serviceable and comfortable and very plain with at most a fold, a bow or a gilt chain across the toe. For day she wears plain black or white court shoes in calf with a high vamp and two-inch cuban heel, for evenings low-heeled slippers in gold or silver kid. Like most women with a lot of walking to do, having found a last and style that suits her she has not altered either. Her heels are now only a very

The all-in-one-colour scheme which makes the Queen so easily picked out in a crowd. Greeting the Duke of Norfolk at Ascot in 1970 she wears a plain tailored dress and coat by Hartnell in her favourite pale blue, with a helmet hat of pale blue silk cord. Simple and unfussy in outline the only decoration is a row of channel seams each side and three self-covered buttons down the front. With this she wears white gloves, white calf bag and shoes, and her daytime jewels which are almost always a necklace of three rows of pearls and pearl stud earrings.

little lower than they were twenty-five years ago: high heels, pointed toes, heavy wedges, platform soles, ankle straps and sling backs are not conducive to comfort for long, and tend to make women walk badly. Not until her U.S.A. visit in 1976 did she venture into high-fashion shoes in kidskin and patent with T-straps.

Head up, hand waving, a charming smile all round after miles and miles of walking, hours and hours of standing, it is a tribute to Edward Rayne who has made her shoes since 1946 that although in private she will kick off her shoes and put her feet up, in public she invariably appears to be walking on air.

The other most important accessory in the Queen's wardrobe are her hats. Although most women do not wear hats any more, these are still an accepted part of dress for every woman for garden parties at the Palace and for Ascot. There have been girls at the garden parties who wore mini-skirts, but they always wore hats. There have been girls in the Royal Enclosure at Ascot who wore trousers, but they always wore hats. Hats are considered appropriate for social dress-up occasions where royalty is present. Hats are ageing, except to the very young, but hats imply formality and the Queen on duty is never without one.

Just as the design of her clothes is shared between three designers, so the design of her hats is shared by three milliners, and each milliner works with one designer.

When Norman Hartnell has made the clothes, Simone Mirman designs the hats to go with them. When it is a Hardy Amies design, Freddie Fox makes the

Around 1966 when she began to find her personal style the Queen discovered that the best hat to suit the royal formula was a small head-hugging turban or beret or helmet shape. It showed her face, it stayed put, it was neat and it was trouble free.
In 1966 (above) she wears the turban style in scarab-blue coq feathers to match her scarab-blue slub silk collar; in 1970 (below) the turban is in the same print as her dress; in 1976 (opposite) she is still wearing it but in a cleaner, clearer line with a knitted wool band round the forehead.

hats. When an Ian Thomas outfit is accepted, it is his own milliner, Valerie, who makes the hats.

And just as each dress designer has an establishment which reflects his style so do the milliners.

Simone Mirman is a Frenchwoman who trained at Schiaparelli, came to England thirty years ago and got her first introduction to the Royal Family when she made hats for Princess Margaret. She has made hats for every member of the Royal Family and treasures a family portrait taken after the birth of Princess Margaret's first baby which shows the Queen, the Queen Mother, Princess Margaret and the baby (in a bonnet of Valenciennes lace) all wearing Mirman hats.

She has made the Queen's hats for her Hartnell clothes since 1965. Her establishment is an imposing house in Chesham Place, the ground floor crammed with hundreds of model hats, and the smallest, most discreet imaginable, brass plate announcing her name on the front door, like a Harley Street consultant's. Though if you look closely you can see an equally discreet 'By Appointment' shield on the window.

Freddie Fox is an Australian who began making the Queen's hats in 1968 when she went to Mexico. His salon is above a flower shop off Bond Street, small, chic, select and, like the salons of all the Queen's suppliers of clothes, frequented by duchesses.

Valerie is the skilful young milliner who works in Ian Thomas's salon and therefore is more closely associated with the dress designs from the beginning.

In general they work on the same principle: when a design for an outfit has been accepted by the Queen, the sketch together with the material is sent to the milliner who prepares several suggestions for suitable hats.

Freddie Fox may take just the shapes to try on, and give several fittings. Simone Mirman who knows the exact size of the Queen's small head will take the completed hats for her to try on, several for each dress. Valerie will discuss the hat with Ian Thomas and get his approval before she takes the model along. The milliner may be present at early fittings and would always be present at the final one.

They all know the royal rules. Hats must be off the face so that people can see the Queen's face.

This was a lesson learnt the hard way by the elegant Princess Marina, who, new to the royal rules, made a mistake which has never since been repeated, and which remains a classic example of how high fashion and royal duty can clash.

Riding in an open carriage on one of her first public appearances in this country, she wore a superbly chic picture hat wreathed in floating ostrich feathers and worn, as it should be, slightly tilted to one side, with the result that the crowd lining one side of the route had an excellent view of her profile, and the crowd on the other side of the route saw only her hat and her arm which constantly had to hold the hat on. The photograph on page 19 also illustrates this point.

Hats must be secure because the Queen must have both her hands free to shake hands or accept a bouquet, and this is usually achieved by two hatpins covered so as to be unnoticeable in the same material as the hat, sometimes with a comb sewn inside the crown, sometimes with a velvet band inside the crown. Veils and long floating trimmings are out: they can blow the wrong way in a wind. Hard hats are out: they are too uncomfortable. Anything too youthful is out. 'I am fifty now' the Queen will remind her dressmakers and her milliners. 'I'm a married woman with grown-up children – not a debutante'. And greatly to their

(above left) The helmet hat made in plaited straw with a little tassel at the back is shown here in a picture taken in 1968. Exactly the same style in silk cord can be seen in the colour illustration facing page 89.
For weddings and garden parties where fussy hats have always been traditional for British ladies the Queen will wear flowers and feathers, but in a far more assured style than when she was younger. At a June Garden Party at Marlborough House in 1968 (above right) the Queen's hat is a neat beret covered with little white flowers; at a wedding in 1967 (below left) she wears the turban style covered with ostrich feathers; and in June 1967 (below right) her hat is a wide wreath of carnations.

distress, large forward tilted hats are out. 'We made for her a beautiful capeline in soft straw' one of them confided ruefully, 'she looked so lovely in it. But no, immediately the scissors were out and we had to cut it down'. Anyone who has seen the photographs of Ascot hats reduced to a floppy mess by a sudden downpour or caught billowing like a sail in a storm must admit that the Queen knows her job.

This is just one more example of the difference between a fashion which is posed and lighted, in the unlikely environs of a fashion studio and the fashion which is meant to be worn. There is a shrewd distinction and a realistic approach which the Queen fully appreciates.

The only large hat which the Queen will wear is the Breton style with an upswept brim which conforms to the royal rules by not being too large and not concealing her face. One of the most successful examples of this style was the hat she wore with her brown-and-white outfit for her arrival in France on her 1972 visit, a dark-brown straw with an upswept brim lined with white.

Quite recently, in pursuit of her economies she has had white straw hats with slots round the crown where scarves of dress material can be threaded through, so that she can change the trimming to match her dress, and turbans which use the same trick and have bands of dress material slotted through the band round her head.

But all conform to the overriding demands of comfort and speed. The Queen is given so little time to fit in appointments in her overseas schedules that she is usually running down the passage as she finishes dressing.

Royal weddings demand a hat which is festive but regal. For Princess Alexandra's wedding the dress and coat (left and right) were in lily-of-the-valley green silk organza with the lily flowers embroidered down the front of the dress; the hat was a skull cap entirely covered with the same little white silk flowers. For Princess Anne's wedding, 14 November 1973, (insert) the Bride's Mother wore bright sapphire-blue silk with a Tudor-shaped hat in the same material edged with sapphire ruched lace.

The smart Breton shape much loved by the Queen made an appearance as long ago as 1965 (above) on her visit to Germany. It was worn with great elan on the visit to America in 1976. She wears the breton style (left) with a swathe of the dress material round the crown, a trimming which can be altered to match the dress. On another occasion (insert) the upturned brim of the straw hat is lined with the same print as the dress.

(opposite) Clear apricot slubbed silk makes another of the effective 'total' look outfits with hat to match photographed at York races in 1972. The turn-back brim shaped like a cuff is faced with the same material as the dress, the coat has no trimmings other than channel tucking down the sides, even the buttons are covered in the same material as the coat so as not to distract the eye, and the stand-up collar is tailored to stand away from the neck and reveal a glimpse of the pearls. The skirt length, just below the knee, is as far as the demands of royal dressing allowed the Queen to go towards the short-skirt fashion – then just going out; the shoes and handbag are in black patent leather.

Another accessory which changes with fashion but not with the Queen is her handbag. Always capacious, always in good quality heavy calf for daytime and sometimes silver tissue for evening, often black and occasionally white, never without a loop to hang over her wrists, and never far from her side, they have ignored fashion change and been a frequent subject of criticism. Almost the only occasions when they are not in evidence is when she is opening parliament. Otherwise the ubiquitous handbag is close beside her, either over her wrist or tucked behind her on a chair.

Clearly the crazes for clutch handbags and shoulder handbags are out of the question, for the Queen must keep both hands free and cannot be bothered with hitching up shoulder bags which continually slip.

But the capacious size of her handbags remains a mystery, for she never has to pay out ready cash, doesn't need the front door key, doesn't smoke, doesn't need a shopping list, doesn't have to pay the grocer's bills out of pocket, and appears to go for hours without renewing her make-up. Any woman who can sit on a horse for one-and-three-quarter hours, with a velours tricorne on her head, buttoned up to the neck in a heavy face-cloth uniform in a searing heat-wave as the Queen has done at the ceremony of Trooping the Colour and never acknowledge the intense heat by the least sign or shine, nor produce the tiniest handkerchief to mop the tiniest bead of perspiration off her brow whilst all around were mopping theirs, any woman who can do that must have little need of constant face repairs.

It must explain why, although she is almost never seen without her handbag, she is never seen to open it. Possibly, as for many women, it is more a psychological support than a practical necessity. The one immutable

(right) The importance of getting the royal accessories right is illustrated by this photograph taken in July 1969. During a visit to an aircraft carrier in Devon the Queen had to negotiate a ship's ladder in a high wind, and with the help of officers from H.M.S. Eagle she checks that her heels are intact.

(opposite) Grouped together at the Investiture of the Prince of Wales in 1969 this picture shows the importance of colour on any occasion where all the Royal ladies appear together, and where the Queen must hold the stage against a clamorous background of brilliant pageantry. The Queen Mother in sharp apple green, Princess Margaret in bright pink, and Princess Anne in a clear turquoise form a background for the Queen in a pale soft primrose coat trimmed with pearls. One of the rare occasions when all accessories were matched to the outfit, gloves, shoes, handbag and parasol in the same pale primrose, the slight figure held the stage against the imposing background of grey Caernarvon Castle, green sward and brilliant uniforms. The hat edged with pearls held an echo of Tudor Queens, and the parasol, one of many kept at Buckingham Palace, was an old one recovered by her milliner, Simone Mirman, in the same heavy silk fabric.

*The unchanging style of the Queen's shoes and handbags
illustrated in these pictures which span the twenty-five
years of her reign. In 1952 (left) the Queen in a coat that is
after Dior – but a long way after – still wears her calf
leather court shoes with peep toes. Nearly twenty years
later (above) she wears in Sydney, Australia the same
court shape, the same cuban heel, perhaps a little lower,
and a closed toe, and a capacious leather handbag with
loop handle. In London three years later (above right) she
wears the same style in black patent with her pale blue coat
and a big black patent leather handbag looped over her arm.
In Boston in 1976 (right) she wears the same style in
white calf with a white calf handbag, looped over her arm.*

*For evenings her usual acces-
sories are silver or gold kid
slippers with a kid or mesh
bag to match, and a stole in
mink, with a selection of the
royal jewels. Here the lovely
triple row of diamonds with
her diamond chandelier earrings.*

detail of design is that there must be a loop handle so that she can slip it over her wrist and forget it.

As for other fashionable accessories, like long football scarves on day dresses or floating triangular chiffon scarves on evening dresses, the Queen will accept the designs but she will seldom wear the scarves unless they are fastened securely. There is too much fussing and hitching involved. And where a coat is a mere accessory and not a fixed, tidy and buttoned part of the outfit, she will not accept that either. One designer, trying to persuade her to wear a loose wrap-around coat, explained that it should be negligently clutched together across the middle. 'And I suppose' she asked mincing in a mannequins' walk across the room, 'that I should walk like this?' Nor will she accept the tie belts which are fussy to knot correctly and have a way of untying themselves.

Gloves which are regarded as essential by the Queen are not only a sign of formality, though rather old-fashioned, but a practical defence for a woman who has in the course of duty to shake so many hands. When the film star Barbra Streisand at a première impertinently and tactlessly asked her why she always wore them, Her Majesty was too polite to give the correct answer which was that she wore them because she had to shake hands with so many people like Barbra Streisand. Although the Queen has perfected a rather limp royal handshake which protects her fingers (some members of the Royal Family have had to have their arms in slings after too much hand-shaking; the Duke of Windsor when Prince of Wales had once to use his left hand), she is further protected by wearing gloves. Although fine suede gloves (which have to be cleaned) are more elegant the Queen prefers gloves in suede fabric, easily washed, easily removed, easily dyed. For someone who may have to put on a hat in a couple of

One other immutable fashion is the royal glove. Long after wearing gloves went out of fashion the Queen continues to wear them for practical reasons and because they add a note of formality. Most often white so the waving hand is easily seen, sometimes dyed to match her shoes, they are of all lengths and in suede fabric. Here dyed coffee brown to go with her white wool coat trimmed with beaver, and as always with the one essential piece of jewellery which governs her life, a wrist-watch worn outside the glove.

seconds, the time consumed in smoothing on suede gloves is something which she cannot afford.

The results of this fixed formula may infuriate fashion pundits, but without it the Queen would need five hands; one to hold onto her hat, one to clutch her handbag, one to hold her coat close, one to receive bouquets or official gifts and one to shake hands.

No one who has travelled with her denies the success of the formula. 'It was over 90 degrees' reports one of the Thai officials who accompanied her in Thailand, 'all our women were dressed coolly in the local fashion in long loosely-wrapped-around skirts, no stockings and no hats. But the Queen sat there wearing her European summer dress, gloves and a hat and looked cooler. I don't know how she did it.'

'You are never conscious of her in relation to her clothes' reported a press photographer who has followed her on many tours, 'she is never fussing with her dress or patting her hair, she sits decorously on platforms above the crowd with never the suggestion of a slip showing. Of course we are on the look out for some untoward incident that would make news, but I have never seen her even powder her nose or look in a hand mirror. She is always completely in charge of herself, and immaculately dressed.'

Another example of the smooth royal performance which impresses everyone who follows a royal progress is the magical way in which the Queen will accept numerous gifts and bouquets and yet is never cluttered with them.

She will accept a gift graciously, open the case and admire the contents, then put it down and move on. Or she will be given a bouquet, thank the giver with a few words and a smile, keep it with her for fifteen minutes, then unobtrusively turn round and hand it on to someone behind her, and walk on. On at least two occasions on the latest visit to the States her Press Secretary found himself holding a bouquet which he somehow managed to pass on to someone else.

'It is a Houdini act' said one reporter admiringly. 'One minute there she is holding the bouquet and the next minute it is gone, without feelings being hurt. At the Lincoln Memorial when she was climbing the long flight of steps someone from among the crowd of Americans, British and Australians lining the steps pressed forward and gave her a posy of flowers. She was still holding it at the top of the steps, but by the time she had walked through the Memorial it had disappeared and on the way down the steps she was handed another posy.'

With the arrival of T.V. covering so many royal appearances the meticulous attention to detail becomes even more demanding. Five hundred million people watched Princess Anne's wedding, and not one of the royals fluffed their part.

THE ROYAL FAMILY ORDERS

Her Majesty normally wears the Orders of King George V and King George VI. The Queen's badges are all made by Garrards. The pictures they contain are painted on ivory by Hay Wrightson. The orders are known to date back to 1820 and George IV, and with the exception of King Edward VIII have been renewed each reign.

George V Family Order

Obverse: Inset within an oval band of large diamonds surmounted by an Imperial Crown with a crimson-enamelled cap, a miniature of His Majesty in the uniform of Admiral of the Fleet wearing the Star and riband of the Garter and the Badge of the Royal Victorian Order.

Reverse: Gold, on a radiated ground in raised letters the Royal Cypher in diamonds, and left and right of it the year of institution, 1911.

Riband: Light sky blue. This riband was chosen as similar to the Royal Guelphic Order of Hanover instituted by King George IV, but which became obsolete in 1837.

George VI Family Order

Obverse: Inset with an oval band of large diamonds surmounted by an Imperial Crown, a miniature of His Majesty in the uniform of Admiral of the Fleet and wearing the Star and riband of the Garter and the Royal Victorian Chain.

Reverse: Gold with the Royal Cypher in raised gold letters and the year of institution, 1937, in raised gold figures, the whole on a radiated ground.

Riband: Rose pink.

Elizabeth II Family Order

Obverse: Portrait of The Queen within a border of brilliants and baguette diamonds. Surmounted by a diamond-set Tudor Crown and three stone diamond loops, resting on a velvet cushion of red enamel. The whole set in platinum. The miniature depicts the head and shoulders of Her Majesty wearing evening dress with the riband and Star of the Order of the Garter. Her earrings are pearl drops. Her necklace is of diamonds – part of a wedding present from the Nizam of Hyderabad.

Reverse: In 18-carat gold, engine-turned in a ray design with the Royal Cypher and St Edward Crown superimposed in gold and enamel. The velvet cushion of the Crown is in red enamel.

Riband: Of watered silk (in a bow) two inches wide in chartreuse yellow.

The badges of these Orders are worn on the left shoulder suspended from bows of the ribands to which are fitted, behind the bows, platinum brooch pins attached to the diamond Imperial Crowns.

The present holders of The Queen's Family Order are: Queen Elizabeth, The Queen Mother; The Princess Anne, Mrs Mark Phillips; The Princess Margaret, Countess of Snowdon; Princess Alice, Duchess of Gloucester; The Duchess of Gloucester; The Duchess of Kent; Princess Alexandra, Mrs Angus Ogilvy; Princess Alice, Countess of Athlone.

In Canberra on her trip to Australia in 1954 the Queen wears a full-skirted gown of pale green tulle over matching silk taffeta with a garland of tea roses on her right shoulder, the Garter sash with the royal miniatures over her left shoulder, a cameo inherited from Queen Victoria on her right hip, the Jubilee necklace and her first tiara.

103

7
The Royal Dressmakers

Behind the smiling pictures of the Queen riding in a car along the Mall beside some visiting dignitary, presiding at a banquet for Commonwealth ministers, putting in her annual appearances at Ascot, garden parties, Maundy Thursday, attending or giving parties on State visits, or waving to crowds in far away countries, behind this smooth and smiling performance which continues year after year lie at least a year's planning ahead, months of fittings, and over twenty-five years of experience and hard work.

"planning a year ahead"

Her wardrobe must stretch to embrace every appearance from a banquet on the Pacific tropical island of Tonga to the inspection of a factory in the sombre environs of Leeds.

The infinite detail which goes into the early planning means that the Queen, better than any other woman, is able to live up to the old maxim that a well-dressed woman having put on her clothes then forgets about them.

In general she prefers to forget that there may be millions of people watching her on T.V. and concentrate on the job in hand. The Investiture of the Prince of Wales was seen by 500 million people, went live to Australia, America, Canada, Japan and Mexico and was translated into thirty-eight foreign languages.

The fact that she can sail through these ordeals with assurance is a tribute not only to her professionalism but to that of the people who make her clothes.

Planning her wardrobe begins at least a year ahead. For her Jubilee year during which she knew she would be exceptionally busy with even less time for fittings, the Queen planned her clothes two years in advance. Fortunately the demands of the royal formula have always meant that she can give only a slight acknowledgment to the latest trends in cut and colour and style. An example of this was at the Investiture of the Prince of Wales at Caernarvon in 1969 when the miniskirt fashion was at its height. The royal skirt was just above the knees, the style (a slim-fitting dress and coat embroidered with pearls) chosen because it was not too lavish but yet appropriate to a Queen on such an occasion, and the colour was a pale primrose yellow because it stood out from the background of vivid green grass and the official robes of scarlet and gold.

The task of designing her clothes falls mainly on three men.

Norman Hartnell made his first dress for the Queen in 1935 and has made clothes for every member of the Royal Family and for practically every important occasion. He makes most of the Queen's opulent, lavish and most queenly evening and state gowns, and his speciality is the exquisite (and uncopiable) embroidery which he designs himself. Until recently his salon employed eighty-five embroideresses. But he also designs and makes many of her daytime outfits, though never her hats.

Hardy Amies who began designing her clothes in 1951 for her Canadian tour when she was Princess Elizabeth, made his name primarily with beautifully-cut and simple tailored clothes in excellent woollens and silks. His evening dresses get their effect more from the cut and the material than from the decoration, and when he uses jewelled embroidery this is done for him by the firm of S. Lock Limited, Royal Warrant holders for many years.

A newcomer to the team is Ian Thomas who used to work for Norman Hartnell. He has been making her clothes for five years and has a more informal approach both to his designs and to his client. His contributions are softer, less dramatic styles which she chooses for her private life where she can allow her personal taste to dictate without the myriad restrictions imposed on

This picture of the Queen at Ascot in 1956 illustrates the problem that her dressmakers face in trying to make clothes for her which will single her out from the crowd. In the early days she relied on pale colours and summery prints, a formula now replaced by the more effective one-colour outfits.

public royal dress. But he too, makes clothes for her to wear on public occasions.

These are only general outlines and the way in which the dressing is shared out is illustrated by the Queen's immensely successful wardrobe for her visit to France in 1972. Paris has so long been regarded as the home of high fashion, and the French are understandably so reluctant to admit the excellence of British clothes that designing for this visit is always regarded as a special challenge.

For her two main gala occasions the Queen chose one dress from Hartnell and one from Amies.

The dress which she wore for the reception given for her by M. Pompidou at Versailles was in delicate orchid-mauve satin, the tight-fitting bodice with elbow sleeves embroidered in pearls and rhinestones, with a matching, tailored, ground-length coat in the same orchid-pink double satin. With this she wore her diamond and pearl tiara, diamond and pearl Jubilee necklace, diamond and pearl drop earrings, and diamond brooch with pearl drops. This dress was made by Amies.

For the reception which she gave to M. Pompidou at the British Embassy, the Queen, as mentioned previously, wore the magnificently elegant slender ground-length coat of white lace on silver tissue edged down the front with white mink, over a slim-fitting dress of silver tissue banded with gold round the hem. With this went the Russian fringe tiara and emerald and diamond necklace, emerald and diamond drop earrings, and diamond bracelets. This dress was made by Hartnell.

She arrived in Paris in Hardy Amies' tailored brown wool coat over a brown-and-white print dress. For an

The dramatic and simple dress in lustrous white and black satin which was a little too dramatic and simple. The idea behind Hartnell's design was that the Queen should be a contrast to the film and stage stars at a Charity Performance in 1953, but the dress was copied and on sale in London stores the next day. It achieved the necessary effect but the Queen was never seen wearing it again.

afternoon reception she wore Hartnell's white silk coat over an orange-and-white pleated silk dress with an orange silk turban.

And Ian Thomas came into the picture too with outfits of a lime-green dress and coat in gaberdine, and a coat in Pervenche-blue-and-white printed silk over a dress in the same pattern in printed georgette.

These three men, together with three milliners, share the task of creating the vast new wardrobes yearly required for a unique job. Precluded from buying like other wealthy women from the chic couturièrs of France, Italy and Spain the Queen's clothes have throughout her life been resolutely British. On the one occasion when Princess Margaret bought a Dior dress the wails of protest from the British fashion trade in this country were so loud that the experiment has never, to public knowledge, been repeated.

Each of the three have their own style of London establishment as well as of design.

Hartnell's salon and work rooms are in a magnificent Georgian house in Bruton Street. The huge showroom is grey and crystal, with mirror walls, grey velvet upholstering the soft seats which line the room, and enormous crystal chandeliers. Amies' salon is in an eighteenth-century house in Savile Row, the home of British tailoring, the showroom in colours of cream and gold, white painted panelling, and gilt chairs.

(far left) Hartnell venturing once again into dramatic black and white for her visit to France in 1957 made an effective outfit of black satin coat with wide white satin revers worn with white petal hat. But it is not a coat that she has worn often.

(left) The beginning of the one-colour outfits in a tailored coat by Hardy Amies in palest aquamarine ottoman silk with cuffs of blonde mink, and a tiny hat of feather pads in aquamarine with tips in deeper blue. The gloves and shoes and handbag are in soft beige.

One ever-present check on following high fashion is the necessity for the Queen to be able to sit decorously on a platform, usually raised above the crowd who have come to see her. Here on a visit to Portugal in 1957 she gives a lesson in how to sit with regal modesty on these occasions.

Ian Thomas works from a small chic boutique off Lowndes Street, where the atmosphere is informal and racks of dresses line the wall.

The Queen, however, has never visited any of the showrooms, except as a small child when she was taken to Hartnell's to try on her first Hartnell gown, a bridesmaid's dress.

The procedure involved in making clothes for the Queen is both lengthy and remarkably formal.

The channel through which the dressmaker communicates with the Queen is the devoted, indispensable, power-behind-the-scenes Miss Margaret Macdonald who fifty years ago was the Queen's nursery maid and is now the all-important Queen's Dresser. Miss Macdonald held the Queen in her arms when she was a baby and is probably closer to her than anyone outside her immediate family. Since she is utterly loyal, never talks about her work, is jealous of the Queen's dignity, is concerned above all with seeing that this part of the Queen's role does not add unnecessarily to the burden of the Queen's job, and moreover is the one responsible for the packing and pressing and correct assembly of the outfits, her advice is never ignored and seldom countered.

The Queen makes all the decisions, writing 'Yes' or 'No' beside each suggested design, she makes them swiftly and she never allows herself the feminine prerogative of changing her mind at the last minute.

But on Miss Macdonald falls the task of organizing, cross-filing, ticketing, maintaining, selecting and laying out with the correct accessories whatever the Queen is to wear, and her presence is assured at every discussion and every fitting.

Each designer's association with the royal client differs slightly, Norman Hartnell being perhaps the most formal and Ian Thomas the least. But the usual form is for Miss Macdonald to write to the designer asking him to prepare some designs for the Queen's clothes in the forthcoming year, which may perhaps include an overseas visit.

The designer then gets from the Palace the diary of events and the itinerary for the journey and the various scheduled appointments she will have. The fact that the same diary will be seen by each designer does not mean that they compete, for there may be as many as four or five different changes of dress in one day.

Once the designer has received the schedule from the Palace and knows exactly what the Queen will be doing and when and where, he sets about the designing, making sketches and selecting suitable swatches of material for each. Although he has special assignments in mind when he designs there is no guarantee that she will wear that particular outfit on that particular occasion. It

The incident which the dressmakers are warned against, the Queen plans against and the photographers wait for. Getting out of a car elegantly is taxing enough, but a sudden gust of wind can be detrimental to royal dignity. This problem, which also means that the Queen needs to concentrate on her skirt rather than her job, has now been eliminated.

(top left) The problem of what to wear when you are a white queen in a sea of black faces, with the womenfolk in gorgeous, vivid colours, was usually solved in Governor's lady style. In cool, print dresses, flowery hats, an example of the true British grit she goes out in the noonday sun with long gloves, leather court shoes, and Ascot handbag.

(top right) One of the hazards which their other clients do not face is that of having their lovely clothes covered in a hairy cloak. Here in New Zealand her carefully designed outfit is more than somewhat marred by the traditional Maori feather cloak which she was expected to wear.

(bottom left) An example of the subtle implications which are taken into account by her dressmakers when she visits a foreign country is illustrated by the design of this dress for the Queen's visit to Japan in 1975. The embroidery of pink cherry-blossom on pale blue (details of the embroidery are on page 88) is a compliment to the famous Japanese cherry-blossom, the kimono sleeves are an echo of the national dress.

(bottom right) The professional good sense behind the Queen's dislike of dark colours is seen clearly in this photograph of the Queen in Washington in 1976. She wears a Hartnell coat in dull thick silk with a slight sheen in ice-white, with a Simone Mirman beret in the same material, and white accessories.

was not until they saw the pictures in the papers that the firm of Amies knew she had selected for her arrival in Philadelphia and for the opening of the Olympic Games the special outfits they had designed for those occasions. As last minute changes in the weather can so often lead to last minute decisions. And the grand dress which Hartnell made for her to wear at a dance in America was abandoned when the Queen found the other guests would be informally dressed, so instead she substituted a simple evening dress in organza.

The designer then sketches his designs and attaches to each sketch patterns of suggested materials. The sketches delineate a vague likeness of the Queen, and although they may include suggested accessories and the outline of a tiara for evening, these details are settled by the Queen.

When the sketches are ready, which will take several weeks according to the number prepared, the designer or his head 'vendeuse' appointed to deal with Her Majesty will ring up Miss Macdonald and ask when it will be convenient to call. The designer together with his head saleswoman or 'première' then calls at the Palace at the appointed time at the Privy Purse entrance, they are met by a footman and escorted to the royal appartments, where they are shown to a waiting room.

Once the Queen has approved the clothes she wants made, they are prepared for the first fitting. As in any top-level dress house there are usually three to four fittings required for each garment, each of which may last half an hour. But in order to lessen the time required from the Queen, her dressmakers try to cut this down to a quarter of an hour. Recently Hartnell has given the Queen a preview of his collection since she is slim enough to try on the model dresses. Indeed so slim, that if she takes a model dress it is removed from the collection so that no one else may have the same dress, and the only alterations needed are shortening to the skirt and taking in the waistline to fit the Queen's twenty-three-inch waist. In any case a session lasts at least two to two-and-a-half hours and usually takes

(left) The first time that the Queen relinquished the full-skirted dresses which were the traditional royal evening dress of the Queen Mother was on her visit to Paris in 1957. She wore her first slinky dress for a trip down the Seine by night. The astonishing beauty of this sheath of shimmering silver and crystal won so much praise for its elegance that the Queen was won over to the new slender line.

(right) Hardy Amies persuaded the Queen into one of her first brilliant colours with this dress in bright peacock-blue faille embroidered in electric blue for her Paris visit in 1957. 'Oh, that's a bright colour' she remarked. 'The brightest, Ma'am, that I have ever suggested' he said. 'But now you are a "femme de trente ans" I think you can wear it'. 'That is the unkindest thing that anyone has said to me today' she replied with a laugh. But she wore it and invited him to see her in it before she left for her appointment.

place in the afternoons generally between 2.30 and 5 pm.

Although the Queen herself has to stand throughout that time, she is tireless and never grumbles or complains, possessing the same kind of tireless energy which enabled her grandmother to walk most of her attendants off their feet.

The fittings are attended by the designer himself, his vendeuse who notes the alterations required, his ladies' tailor who is responsible for silk coats and skirts, his man's tailor who makes the woollen tailored clothes, and his dress fitter. At the final fitting the milliner will also be there. They go to the tradesmen's entrance because it is not permitted to carry clothes through the Palace.

All of them curtsey or bow on entering the fitting room, stand throughout (except for the men who retire and sit down while the Queen changes) and all bow and curtsey at the end of the session and back out of the room to the waiting room where there is generally tea

provided for them – and at Christmas time a special Christmas tea.

At the halfway stage the clothes are first unpacked in the waiting room and hung on rails ready to be wheeled in to the fitting room. When they are finished they are taken to the Palace on hangers in special clothes covers made for the Queen in opaque material so that the secret of what the Queen will wear shall not be revealed.

In the Queen's fitting room there are a dressing table and large triple mirrors, so that she can walk, turn, sit and see herself from the front, from the back, and from the side.

And in the corridor connecting the waiting room with the fitting room are huge cupboards, one reserved for Hartnell's clothes and one for Amies', another instance of the professionalism and the courtesy which the Queen maintains, for it ensures that there is no slight and no hitch involved by confusing them.

(far left and left) The submitted sketches, in line with the proper procedure for royal dress designers, shows a likeness but not a portrait of the royal client. Her newest and youngest dressmaker, Ian Thomas made for the Queen this dress in peach-coloured crepe (left). Succeeding against a long-established royal formula he gave the dress huge swirling crystal pleated sleeves embroidered down each pleat with crystal gold and topaz. (far left) Sketch by Hardy Amies for a private order of a very simple tailored evening dress in bright pink ottoman silk.

(opposite) One of her favourite dresses, one made for the successful tour of the U.S.A. in 1976 and one that illustrates the recent changes from stiff formal fabrics into soft and flowing and very feminine materials. In peach-coloured chiffon, the bodice is embroidered in gold, peach and topaz 'jewels'; fastened to the shoulders in front are two wings of peach chiffon which cover the arms and flow away to the hem at the back. With it she wears her silver kid slippers and silver kid portmanteau-shape evening bag. Made for her by Ian Thomas who makes many of the clothes she wears for private entertaining, this is a dress which without the regal jewels, she could wear for grand occasions 'at home'.

8
In Private Life

For any woman who has had for over thirty years to wear formal clothes, to wear hundreds and hundreds of them, to pay meticulous attention to every detail, to have endless discussions with dressmakers and endless fittings, to have to choose always on the basis only of suitability for the job in hand, the infrequent chance to wear what she pleases presents a relaxation and a temptation.

"my husband and I"

The temptation to be careless or carefree about what she wears is clearly, judging from all existing pictures and from all first-hand reports, firmly resisted. The Queen is as carefully turned out, though in a different style, when she is walking the corgis at Sandringham as she is when opening parliament at Westminster. The long training in careful dressing carries her as correctly through the mud as through the reception line.

Her relaxations, whether watching her horses in training or the Badminton horse trials or Ken Dodd, Kojak and Morecambe and Wise on T.V., demand informal clothes, but they are always impeccable. Once a woman has learnt this polished technique, as many a top-flight model girl proves, the finish is always there. Once a Queen, always a Queen. 'Whenever I have seen her' one student of the royal clothes remarked, 'she looks just as a Queen should look.'

One of the most delightful informal pictures ever taken of the Queen shows her as her subjects seldom see her, and was taken for her silver wedding when she was forty-six years old. With her hair blown by the wind instead of immaculately groomed, wearing sun-glasses which would so obviously disappoint the crowds who had come to get a close view of her, she leans over the side of the Royal Yacht. In place of the gallant social smile there is a hearty laugh, instead of the formal clothes a sleeveless dress with the collar blowing in the wind, and a camera slung round her neck.
The dress has a shirt-neck collar edged with white rick-rack braid and a pattern of formal flowers in pink, blue, black and mauve. Even the pearl necklace is gone and the only jewels are tiny stud earrings, a wrist watch, and her wedding and engagement rings.

The conservative approach imposed on her by her early background, her training and her own rigid sense of propriety has been a long time dying. Accustomed to play safe and usually proved right, it is only within the last few years that she has taken a real interest in clothes, shown a keener eye for fashion, ventured a little more bravely into different styles, and received genuine compliments from those who understand fashion. Her evening dresses always merited President Truman's compliment 'a fairytale Princess', but fairytale princesses do not have to trudge round housing estates and there is no precedent for the right clothes for them to wear in Crawley New Town in the rain.

The praise from discriminating critics which greeted her latest tours to France in 1972, to Japan in 1975 and to the States in 1976 was the result of her new personal enthusiasm. Previously she heard 'How regal', 'How beautiful', 'How magnificent'. Lately, even from the grudging French, it was 'Quelle élégance'.

To her new image she must owe much to her children, always a woman's severest and most outspoken critics, who have been more in the swing of current taste than ever she was allowed to be. The first joke she ever made in public was in her speech at a celebration lunch at the Guildhall for her silver wedding when she opened with the well-worn phrase so often guyed in earlier days: 'I think everyone will concede' she said with a smile, 'that on this of all days I should begin my speech with the words "My Husband and I".' It could have been written by her wise-cracking son. And it could be due to the influence of a daughter with modern views, a modern approach to the role of monarchy and a great many contacts with the world outside palaces, that the Queen pays more heed to modern fashions.

Another incentive is her figure, slimmer now at fifty than she has ever been, she is a size twelve by current dress sizing, with a smaller-than-size-twelve waist. The Princess who was once in tears because she was plump is now a Queen who is a dress designer's dream.

At her private dinner parties among friends she wears the current styles that any un-royal well-dressed woman would wear, the kind of clothes that fashion experts are always urging on her and which do not require or permit a lavish show of royal jewels.

She will wear in the evening separates like a silver tissue skirt banded in black velvet with a black velvet top, or a simple tailored dress and high-necked jacket to match in stiff silk, or a shirt-neck evening dress in floating printed chiffon. Sometimes these gentler, softer, simpler dresses will overflow into some of her queenly appearances like the diaphanous chiffons, the trailing medieval sleeves, the strappy shoes which she wore for the first time on her latest foreign visits.

Her main private interest, apart from her family, is of course training and breeding race horses, although, we are assured, not backing them.

She has proved an exceptionally successful owner financially, and it is a source of pride that although she has proved her ability to carry out the highly paid career which was forced upon her, she also has the knowledge and expertise to earn good money in the open market.

It is probably horses, not diamonds, which are a Queen's best friend. Subject to a continual searchlight and eager eavesdropping she can whisper sweet nothings to a horse. Horses don't write memoirs.

For her country clothes she will buy Daks skirts from Simpsons which are fitted for her at the Palace, and cashmere sweaters and cardigans from Scotland. She wears head-scarves which must be a relief after all those dutiful hats, silk and cotton open-neck shirts, trousers on the Royal Yacht, riding breeches, fur-lined bootees or Wellingtons or brogues, lisle or wool stockings, tweed or camel coats or car coats, and Gannex macintoshes or Burberry coats.

They have little or nothing to do with fashion and have not altered over the years either for her or for any other woman; they are almost exactly the same as the tweed suits and sweaters and shoes she wore as a child.

For summer there are cotton frocks often sleeveless, and plain wool frocks and flat-heeled pumps, and yet the string of pearls, the pearl stud earrings, and the lapel brooch are almost always present.

The people who supply her clothes for her private as well as her public life are all Royal Warrant holders. Any firm which has supplied the Queen to her satisfaction for three years can apply to the Lord Chamberlain for the Royal Warrant and if it is granted display the Royal Arms on their premises and on their writing paper, although they are forbidden to make use of the privilege for advertising. The prestige conferred is good

(opposite) The Queen in the comfortable, but always immaculate, clothes which must be a relief after so much formal finery. Wearing an Arran thick-knit sweater over a Harris tweed skirt, with dark glasses and a camera like any tourist, she is laughing at some competitors in difficulties at the water hazard in the European Driving Championship at Windsor.

It is a penalty of being Royal that there are so many dignified occasions when she would like to laugh outright, but international entente compels her to remain unmoved.

A gallant effort to help at a charity sale of work organised by her mother near Balmoral in 1955 shows the Queen very simply dressed in a print frock, though still with a hat, also the near impossibility of her ever mixing naturally with the crowd. All eyes are on the saleswoman, not the goods.

*In the grounds at Sandringham and at Windsor the tweed
suits she wears in private show a preference for checks and
pleated skirts with easy fitting jackets, over a cashmere
sweater, worn with lisle or wool stockings and fleece-lined
boots or brogues. The slightly more formal version
photographed with her two younger sons at Buckingham
Palace (right) is in ruby-red and charcoal wool.*

116

Taken when Prince Charles was seven in Windsor Great Park her simple cotton dress could, and probably did, come off the peg, for she used at one time to buy clothes from Horrocks. But her sensible walking shoes probably came from one of the world's most expensive shoemakers, Lobb of St James's, and she wears her triple pearl necklet with pearl-stud earrings.

(right and overleaf) A far cry and a welcome relief, at times, from the splendour of her grand state-occasion clothes are these casual country coats in camel and tweed and brushed wool. Instead of a tiara, a head scarf; instead of a necklace, a square of silk; flat-heeled shoes, and no Queenly gloves – the accepted gear for watching horse trials at Badminton and Windsor.

118

(right) It is no mean fashion achievement for a woman to be a knockout in an elaborate evening dress and jewels, and to look stunning too in a tweed riding jacket and open-neck shirt. That she can wear these neat, severe lines, so well, is one reason why she can carry off with assurance the uniform she wears at Trooping the colour.

for trade: 'The Royal Family' said one, 'generally know where to find the best'.

All three dressmakers and milliners are Royal Warrant holders, so are the shoemakers, corsetière, hairdresser and cosmetic supplier, and there is an accredited supplier of hosiery, perfume, dry cleaning, handbags, fur cleaning and moth-proofing. There is also a firm holding the Queen Mother's Royal Warrant as Pin Makers and Manufacturers of Hooks and Eyes, a small but essential part of the Queen's speedy dressing.

It also says much for the Queen's strong-willed dieting that there are royal purveyors of potted shrimps, pork sausages, and creamed horse-radish.

The Queen's practical mind and acute perception of the commercial advantage, which the Royal Warrant bestows, has in the past operated to her own disadvantage. Each firm, conscious of its special privilege, would require a separate interview which the Queen granted. But it made the co-ordination of dress, hat and accessories extremely hazardous: to choose a hat from one designer, a dress from another, the belt from someone else, handbag and shoes from yet another, did not make for a harmonious ensemble and was the despair of her dress designers. 'We would do anything to help her' one of them remarked ruefully some years ago, 'if only she would let us.'

Fortunately the individual warrant holders for her clothes have agreed to work more closely together with more satisfactory results.

Many magnificent furs have been presented to the Queen over the years, but she is seldom seen wearing them today. Perhaps because her husband is President of the World Wild Life Fund she is sensitive to criticism, but the mink coats and jackets of former years are not

(*left and right*) *This evening dress by Hardy Amies, china blue and white embroidered with white beads and gold thread and diamonds in a design of sheaves of corn, was designed for Her Majesty's visit to the Schloss Brühl in the Wittelsbach colours. In double satin covered with silk organza it can with less imposing jewels be worn for a private function.*

often on view or renewed, she never wears leopard skin or seal; at most there is a white or pale mink trimming or a white mink stole made from animals specially bred on farms.

In assessing the Queen's private clothes it must be remembered that she is one of the very few women in the world who never gets a complete holiday. It is not only that wherever she goes, even during her two months' holiday at Balmoral, she is never free from despatches, letters and papers to sign from her ministers and representatives abroad, but she is never free to step outside the grounds without possibly meeting a press photographer.

The constant reminder of her role is always with her whether she is going to the local church or helping to sell goods in a local fête, so that even her most informal appearances are not all that informal.

Even in the B.B.C. film which has made the bravest attempt yet to show the Queen off duty and where she was shown taking Prince Edward to the local sweet shop, the cameramen and technicians were there too, and the informality was staged. It is some measure of the care with which she guards her private life (fiercely helped by her husband who warns off photographers in colourful language) that there has only been one picture of her in a swimsuit taken when she was a schoolgirl.

Still, it must be a holiday for a woman so rigidly disciplined in what she wears on duty not to have to wear a hat, a tiara or a pair of white gloves.

It is not until her standards of dress are compared with an older generation of royals that the enormous generation gap, quite as wide as any that exists among her subjects, can be appreciated.

Three of the new floating chiffon dresses which the Queen loves to wear for private as well as public occasions. (left) Ian Thomas made the brilliant violet and turquoise chiffon with floating wings reaching to the hem; (right) Hartnell's is in a print of pink, lilac and orange, with a cowl neckline and flowing trumpet sleeves; (far right) Amies designed the multi-coloured chiffon dress which falls from the neck in two capes.

Two dresses by Ian Thomas
as sketched by Robb: (far
left) is his dress in pink lilac
and white organza over white
with pleated ruffles falling
from one shoulder and con-
tinuing round the hem, and
(left) a dress in turquoise-
blue silk-crepe with white
crepe pagoda sleeves embroidered in turquoise and crystal.

In her autobiography, *Crowded Life*, Lady Cynthia Colville, who was Woman of the Bedchamber to Queen Mary for thirty years, reports that she made her first social error soon after her appointment. Queen Mary informed her that they would be going to tea with Queen Alexandra at Sandringham, so Lady Cynthia put on her best dark green cloth coat and dress with a hat to match, assuming that they would walk the couple of hundred yards from York Cottage. 'The Queen', wrote Lady Cynthia 'suddenly appeared, and said "But you can't go in a hat!" Her Majesty was dressed as for a party in cloth-of-silver and hatless.' They drove off in a carriage for tea with Queen Alexandra who was in a magnificent tea gown with her Maid of Honour in pale grey crêpe-de-chine. At Buckingham Palace the King wore a frock coat in the daytime and so did the men of the Household as well as ministers and other visitors.

'Almost every night when in London the King and Queen dined alone or with their children in their private apartments. The King wore a tail coat and the Garter and the Queen always put on a tiara for dinner.'

It is not surprising that, with this example before her, the woman within the Queen is so seldom glimpsed: that the carefully stage-managed image reveals so little of the warm, jolly, vivacious and well clued-up personality of her real self.

That she is well clued-up was vouched for by Harold Wilson who said that she often caught him out by knowing more of the subject under discussion than he did; and once having delivered some lovely new dresses one of her designers asked if she would now change into one of them. 'Oh no' she said, 'I shall sit here in what I've got on and do my homework.'

There are so many small anecdotes about the warmer, more sympathetic private side; the time she helped an elderly, distinguished but inebriated guest to bed by putting him in a wheelchair in order not to embarrass him in front of the staff; the times she throws back her head in a hearty belly-laugh; the way she never fails to remember and try to help in any domestic misfortune among those who work for her; the times she saves the little posies of wild flowers given by children (the big bouquets are sent to hospitals) and puts them on her dressing table; all the unreported moments when she permits herself to show the feelings she has trained herself not to reveal in public; the times she has felt like laughing or crying but regal training has prevented her.

Norman Hartnell treasures among all his memories of the resoundingly successful ceremonial affairs in which he has played such a big part a small incident which occurred outside the fitting rooms in Buckingham Palace.

He had been very ill and this was his first attendance on the Queen after he had had a serious operation. Always a stickler for protocol he was standing in the corridor waiting to be summoned when the Queen sent a message asking him to come in and sit down because he was still not fit. Knowing that this was not correct procedure, he refused. Finally he was persuaded to come into the fitting room and sat down, protesting. She dragged up a chair and sat down beside him. 'There, Mr Hartnell' she teased, 'does that make you feel better?'.

It may be argued that the personal charisma which wins the admiration, affection and devoted loyalty of those who work closely with her should be a little more on show to the public, that too much formality still hedges the Queen. But it is questionable whether a more relaxed, more contemporary attitude to her role, and therefore to her clothes which are the outward sign of her approach, could be as successful.

Today fashion has caught up with her. After years which embraced tremendous swings from tight-waisted to waistless, from hatty hats to no hats, from disciplined military lines to do-as-you-please, the cycle has come full circle and today it is once again fashionable to look like a lady.

In terms of clothes the Queen has always done her own thing with a standard of professionalism which makes it unlikely that any successor will ever do it quite so well.

Acknowledgments

Among books consulted were:

Our Princesses and their Dogs, Michael Chance, (John Murray) 1936

Crowded Life, Lady Cynthia Colville, (Evans Brothers) 1963

Footprints in Time, John Colville, (Collins) 1976

The Queen's Life, Heather and Graham Fisher, (Robert Hale) 1976

Silver and Gold, Norman Hartnell, (Evans Brothers) 1955

The Queen's Jewellery, Sheila Young, (Ebury Press), 1968

Illustration sources:

Acknowledgments to colour illustrations are in italics

Hardy Amies: 110 (left)

Camera Press: 10, 13, 20, 25, 30–31, 35, 40, 55, 61, 63 (left), 70 (below left), 82 (left), *opposite 88*, 91, 95 (both), 96 (left), 96 (centre), *opposite 97*, 98, 99 (above left), 99 (below right), 110 (above left), 110 (above right), 110 (below left), opposite 110, *opposite 112*, *opposite 113*, 116 (left), 116 (right), 117, 118–19, 120 (both), 121 (below), 123, 125 (right), 128.

The Daily Express: 8, 18–19 (above), 28, 38 (above right), 63 (above right), 63 (below right), 70 (above right), 70 (below right), 77, 83, 84 (left), 84 (right), 85 (above), 85 (below), 86, *opposite 89*, 90 (above), 90 (below), 93 (above left), 93 (below left), 93 (below right), 96 (right), *opposite 96*, 99 (above right), 100, 102, 109, 110 (below right), 114, 121 (above), 125 (left)

Ian Thomas: 110 (right)

Keystone Press Agency: 101

The Press Association: 36 (above left), 36 (below), 52 (above), 52 (below left), 97

The Radio Times Hulton Picture Library: 12 (above left), 12 (above right), 12 (below), 13, 16, *opposite 16*, *opposite 17*, 18 (below), 19 (below), 21, 22, 23, 24, 26, 27, 29 (above), 29 (below), *opposite 32*, 34, 36 (above right), 38 (below left), 39, 41, 42, 43, 44, 45, 46–47, *opposite 48*, 52 (below right), 54, 57, 58, 59, 60 (left), 60 (right), 64 (above), 64 (below), *opposite 64*, 70 (above left), *opposite 81*, 82 (centre), 82 (right), 103, 104, 107, 108 (above left), 108 (above right), 108 (below), 115, 118

Sport and General Press Agency: 31

Derrick Witty: *reverse of frontispiece, frontispiece, opposite 33, opposite 49, opposite 65, opposite 72, between 72–73, opposite 73, opposite 80, between 88–89*